The subtitle of this story collection, *Telling Stories*, proves this author's craft of telling stories to you that are also telling for you. Buckle up tight as her short, smooth non-fiction explores the highs and lows of life. She will pull you in and leave you emotionally changed.

Critical Praise for *Skating on the Septic Tack*

"*Skating on the Septic Tank* is a collection of compelling stories that will make you smile, cry, and laugh. Genie Smith Bernstein has captured the essence of family and friendship in timeless fashion." ~ Patricia Bell-Scott, author of *The Firebrand and the First Lady: Portrait of a Friendship: Pauli Murray, Eleanor Roosevelt, and the Struggle for Social Justice*

"In the world of Southern storytellers, Genie is one of the best. She blankets the page with description and allows the reader to walk the journey. Everyone must experience our extraordinary South through Genie's eyes." ~ Judith Garrison, editor and writer

"These are miniature novels superbly crafted by a writer of immense talent. Influenced by her experience with magazines, they read smoothly and quickly, yet leave a lingering of delight, or a tremor of melancholy." ~ Terry Kay, author of *To Dance with the White Dog*

"Genie has a special gift of being one of Georgia's great story tellers. She evokes emotion with every story she tells. Her words make us smile, laugh, and sometimes even shed a tear. Genie's contributions to Georgia Connector magazine are invaluable and are anticipated by our readers with each issue." ~ Kenny Smiley, publisher of *Georgia Connector*

ACKNOWLEDGMENTS

I thank God for letting me be born in the *Briarpatch*. The influence of growing up in Putnam County, Georgia, produced these stories. There I was nurtured in the shadows of Joel Chandler Harris, Alice Walker, and Flannery O'Connor. There I had the privilege of learning from teachers who really taught. There a bookmobile filled my summers with reading.

Thank you to all my family and friends for unfailing love: husband, children, grandchildren, great-grandchildren, siblings, cousins, and those who have passed on. You make me whole.

To the many encouragers who fill my writing life: Patricia Bell-Scott for giving me spirit, members of the Harriette Austin Writers Studio for skilled critiques, Kim Wentworth for advice and her sharp editing pencil, girlfriends like Liz Justus and my Keepers group for grounding me, Old Birds coffee group for buoying me up, and my Truthseekers Sunday School class for prayers. I can't imagine being without any of them.

Special thanks to Georgia Connector Magazine, its publisher Kenny Smiley and editor Judy Garrison. These stories would still be hidden within me without the Connections column. There aren't enough words to thank you for the readership and following you give me.

Humble thanks to beloved author Terry Kay for his splendid foreword. He left me speechless.

Skating
on the
Septic Tank

Telling Stories

Genie Smith Bernstein

Genie Smith Bernstein

A Black Opal Books Publication

DEDICATION

To my parents, whom I appreciate more every day.
Sally Callaway Smith
and
Roy Clyde Smith

Foreword

By Terry Kay

We all know such people. The phone rings and we see the name on the Caller ID screen and a kind of gladness leaps up in our spirits. We know there will be no beating around the bush. Before a greeting is spoken, the caller will be word-deep into the sharing of something seen or heard, something having a pendulum swing of hilarity to pathos, for the caller is one of those people with a gift of observing, and the sharing he or she offers will be from language that transforms speech into literature.

Genie Smith Bernstein is one of those people. She reveals it in her collection, *Skating on the Septic Tank*. And she proves it in the subtitle: *Telling Stories*.

There are people who will think of these stories as a hybrid of blogs, but that would do them a disservice. These are miniature novels superbly crafted by a writer of immense talent. Influenced by her experience with magazines, they read smoothly and quickly, yet leave a lingering of delight, or a tremor of melancholy. It's a trick as well as a talent: find the core of the story and write about it without wasting time on 'author' posturing. Genie Smith Bernstein could teach classes on that subject.

In this collection, you will find a fascinating assortment of life events, some in word-snapshots, some in word-portraits. Thankfully, none of the inclusions resort to the cliché of regional caricature that many writers rely on for attention. Instead, the author chooses to celebrate the soul of the moment and in that delicate balance, she soars above the average.

Read *Skating on the Septic Tank*. You might imagine you've just heard your phone ringing and you check the Caller ID screen and you see the name Genie Smith Bernstein.

If that's the case, answer. You'll be glad you did.

Terry Kay, Georgia Hall of Fame, Southeastern Library Association Outstanding Author of the Year, Appalachian Heritage Writers Award, Author of sixteen books, including:

To Dance with the White Dog ~ made into a Hallmark Hall of Fame television movie starring Hume Cronyn and Jessica Tandy.

The Valley of Light ~ Townsend Prize for Fiction

After Eli ~ Georgia Author of the Year Award

Run Down the Rabbit teleplay ~ Southern Emmy Award

Table of Contents

Introduction

The sub-title of this story collection is *Telling Stories* and comes from my sincere desire to tell stories *to* you as well as telling them *for* you. The sum of what I have been exposed to, what I have seen, where I have been, what I have heard, and what I have read, comes out of me in the form of stories. I hope they will be telling for you, as well, be they fiction, non-fiction, or somewhere in between.

When I became a writer after retirement, my friends were perplexed asking, "Why would you want to do that?"

Now that I have published a novel, have had two decade's worth of stories and essays in magazines, and am now putting together this story collection, they've taken the same tone, saying again, "Why would you want to do that?"

The answer hasn't changed. Nothing makes me happier than telling stories. That's part of my psyche, who I am, a key factor in how I live, how I treat people, how I perceive God. The Bible is, at the heart, an anthology.

Join me and enjoy my effort…

       * to entertain and share

       * to teach and learn

       * to get words safely on the page before they are diluted

       * to get intrusive phrases out of my head

       * to connect and communicate

Section I

When I do a creditable piece of writing,
it gives me a sense of self-worth.
Pauli Murray

Chapter 1

Southern Hospitality

When I grew up in Willard, Georgia, a stranger in the neighborhood was an event.

"My Lord, what is that?" Mama came rushing out of the kitchen one hot August day in 1952, drying her hands on her apron as the screen door slapped shut. Four years old, I ran to stare off the end of the porch with her. Brother and our cousin, Little Billy, had just run out of caps and turned their pistols on me, so my bubble game was over anyway. I loved to swipe a wet spool across a bar of Ivory Soap and see how many bubbles I could get to land on Daddy's spread-out army blanket. As soon as Mama spied the contraption in our lane, she shooed us inside with her.

Our noses were pressed against the screen when the biggest horse I'd ever seen snorted and stomped around the side of the well-house. It was pulling a real covered wagon, straight out of a cowboy show. The canvas top puffed out like a big-headed toadstool after a spring rain. The whole outfit wallowed back and forth, clattered to a halt, and scared a week's worth of laying out of Mama's hens. Bohuncus, our happy hound dog, yelped like his tail got stepped on and ran under the porch.

"Whoa, Dolly," a voice shot out from beneath the driver's old-fashioned sunbonnet.

Mama reached up and latched the screen door. It was nearly a hundred degrees, but she crossed her arms and shivered like it was cold. I slid over to the dining room window to peek under the red gingham curtain. The woman who scampered down from the wagon seat looked like a monkey wearing a hand-me-down dress. She tied the reins to the wagon wheel and shook a cloud of red dust out of her clothes. Her long-sleeved blouse was faded so many shades of blue it looked almost white in places.

"Name's Abigail Hamilton." She said it sharp, like driving a nail, with the same twang as our new doctor who Brother said came from up North. "Like to pass the night under yon tree." She pointed to our famous oak tree, the one with the lollipop head you see all the way from town.

Mama loved for folks to stop by. She'd whip off her

apron, pour a pitcher of iced tea, and be offering black walnut fudge before they got in the yard good. It wasn't like her to talk through the screen door in a voice as tight as the knot in her sash. But that's what she did. "You'll have to ask my husband when he gets home."

"Obliged for water," the woman said, and before Mama could say not to, she snatched our aluminum dipper off the well-house post. She took a big swig in her mouth, then spewed it out. "Your water is bad! That stuff'll kill you."

Seven-year-old Billy, with the same bold-faced logic he grew up to use in business, said, "We drink that water, and we ain't dead." A scowl from Mama sent Little Billy scurrying. Brother, nine, the oldest child home that day, stayed glued to Mama.

Out in the county by itself, our farmhouse was a hodge-podge of added on rooms with a wide wrap-around porch, home to lots of Daddy's family before us. Ten steps of handmade bricks led up to the kitchen side of the porch. By the time Miz Hamilton got on the third step, Mama had her arm around Brother, and by the sixth the skin on her fingers turned white. Just before a dirty brogan hit the top step, Mama blurted out, "I don't want you up on my porch."

The woman sidestepped to the buttress and stood stone still. Bohuncus growled from under the porch. Her face was streaked and wrinkled as old leather boots and her eyes, mostly hidden by the bonnet brim, were empty as a chicken's. "I do believe you're a-feared of me," she cackled.

"Yes, Ma'am," Mama said in her tight voice, "I do believe I am."

Right then Daddy drove up the hill in the *Old Black Roach*, his '48 Chevy. Miz Hamilton didn't know about my daddy. He went to work before the sun came up and wasn't friendly when he got home 'til he'd had his cornbread and buttermilk. He strode across the yard with lunch pail in one hand and the Macon Telegraph in the other. He barely noticed the horse and wagon.

"Name's Abigail Hamilton." She stopped him with her spiky voice. "God-fearing woman from Illinois called to bring the gospel to Florida. Like to pass the night under yon tree."

Daddy hadn't paid her horse and wagon no mind, but her smell was a lot like Bohuncus after he'd been swimming in the branch. Waving her off with the newspaper, Daddy said, "Under the tree." He tugged on the screen door and waited while Mama unlatched it.

The wagon woman said, "What church you go to?"

"Baptist," Daddy answered, but didn't look at her. He just came inside and banged the door shut.

"People last week were Baptist," she muttered. "They were rude, too."

Mama latched the screen behind Daddy and went to fix his buttermilk. "Honey," she declared, "some folks in this world you don't want a thing to do with, and that's one of them."

I stayed at my curtain until Brother and Little Billy talked our way back out on the porch. Miz Hamilton tied Dolly to the scuppernong arbor and dug in her hoof with a big knife. "Whoa," she yelled when the horse reared way up over her head.

Brother and Little Billy explored behind the wagon while Mama wasn't looking, and Miz Hamilton went about setting up her wash tub. She smiled at me and held out a bar of brown soap. I wondered what color bubbles it would make. I was all the way to the rub board by the time Sister got home from her after school job. She snatched me away from the tub and called the boys to supper.

While we were washing up, Brother said, "That old woman said she prayed for a horse and wagon and God gave her one."

"That's a lie," Little Billy scoffed, slinging his hands dry. "If we prayed for a horse and wagon, God wouldn't give us one."

They dashed to the table, saying there was a dog inside the wagon, along with skinned rabbits and a sack they just knew was full of snakes. Daddy made them hush up and eat.

The wagon was too close to our double plank swing in the oak tree for me and Sister to sit there after supper and sing *Found a Peanut*. We sat in a porch rocker and

counted lightning bugs while Brother and Little Billy
tried to call up a whippoorwill in the yard. Bohuncus only
came out long enough to eat. After dark, a kerosene lantern inside the wagon made its top glow like a new moon.

"I won't sleep a wink with that thing out there,"
Mama declared.

Daddy went to bed like usual, but she set up her sewing machine at the window. With one eye on the shadows
outside, she took out her patterns and sent us to bed. By
the time we got up the next morning, she had finished
three new school dresses for Sister, all hemmed, pressed,
and hanging on the curtain rod.

Daddy had already left for work and Mama was
wearing her pretty pink sundress with pinafore ruffles
running around the top. She hadn't unlatched the screen
door, and we knew better than to ask about going outside.
Looking like it belonged in a storybook, the big horse
was hitched up to the wagon.

Mama fixed pancakes for Brother and Little Billy.
Sister sliced a banana in cream and sprinkled sugar on top
for me. Before we finished our breakfast Miz Hamilton
came up on the porch and rapped on the door. We all
jumped and Mama, sitting at the head of the table next to
the door, dropped her spoon on the floor. "What do you
want?" Mama said.

"I want to talk to you." The woman yanked on the
door handle and jarred the latch.

"Talk from out there," Mama said, not getting up, and not looking at her.

Miz Hamilton stood there a long time. The bonnet was tied under her chin, but it was pushed down in back. Her eyes were dark and flat as mud pies. My stomach felt funny, and I wanted to cry. She stopped staring through the door at Mama and started staring through the window at us--me and Brother and Little Billy and Sister--having our breakfast like we did every morning without her watching. I edged down the bench closer to Sister.

The woman turned to Mama and said in a thin, ugly voice, "I don't hold with womenfolk showing their arms." She whirled off the porch like a dust devil, and we caught a flash of the big knife she was hiding in the folds of her skirt. She jumped up on the wagon seat, snapped the reins like firecrackers, and rattled away. Brother and Bohuncus ran to the bottom of the hill and watched until she was out of sight.

Right after school started that year, Daddy read about a woman named Abigail Hamilton who got caught stealing a little girl my same age down in Florida.

ℰ∽ℰ∽

I soon forgot about Miz Hamilton, or so I thought. Forty years later, my teenage son waved the local newspaper at me and mumbled around a mouthful of black walnut fudge, "Mom, take a look. Here's that dude you

were so rude to." The picture was of a young man indicted for five horrific ax murders in our city, the same wild-
haired youth who had come to our door the summer before. It had been a hundred-degree day, but staring into
his muddy, flat eyes, I went cold. I cut off his magazine-
selling spiel, the same one he would use to gain entrance
to his victims' homes, by slamming the door smack in his
face.

"Honey," I told my boy, "some folks in this world
you don't want a thing to do with, and that's one of
them."

Chapter 2

Yellow and Gold

The first daffodils of spring fill my heart. Blooms have already opened near my mailbox here in Athens and probably in every yard where I have ever lived. They come from the zillion heirloom bulbs my aunt planted about 1920 on the Roy Smith Homeplace in Putnam County.

The year I was five, I spent long afternoons picking daffodils there while watching for the bus to bring Sister and Brother home from school. Mama, who referred to me as her golden-haired child, named my flower-collecting game "Yellow and Gold" and kept a close eye on me moving from one bright yellow patch to another. I loved to cradle my hand around the bright single trumpet

blooms, and also the vintage clustered variety called butter 'n eggs. I worked my fingers down their fat stems and
broke them off close to the ground. They always made a
nice crunchy sound and exuded a fresh green scent.

Seeing our porch turn yellow with my water-filled
Mason jars of daffodil bouquets, Mama got the idea of
Daddy building me a flower stand. He set it up near his
woodwork shop at the end of the driveway, added a sign
for my wares and a stack of newspapers for me to wrap
my sales. Mama tied my golden curls back with a blue
ribbon and let me play Yellow and Gold to my heart's
content, but she worried I'd be disappointed if no one
stopped to buy my beautiful flowers.

All afternoon cars sped by on their way to Atlanta
without giving me so much as a glance. Finally, a big,
shiny black car pulled off the road. A smiling man
dressed in a fine suit got out and bought a bouquet of daffodils for the lady with him. Then he bought another, and
another, and another, and another. He waited patiently for
me to wrap the stems of each bunch before he carefully
handed the flowers to his companion. I don't remember
what he paid. All I remember is how happy he made the
lady, Mama, and me.

In the final spring of Daddy's life, I opened a little
envelope from him one afternoon as I strolled back from
the mailbox. Unsigned and written in his obviously fail-
ing hand, his note simply said, "The daffodils are bloom-
ing, and I think of you."

Chapter 3

Eye of Sole

Neuroma," the podiatrist diagnosed my recent foot pain. He went on to ask if I remembered a childhood trauma in that spot. Sure, I do, as clear as the eye on the sole of my foot.

I am one of the chosen few ever to stare at the bottom of their foot and find it staring back. No joke. A perfectly round eyeball bigger and bluer than the ones in my head. Beautiful. Hand-blown glass. A relic from some vintage doll, lurking in our farmhouse yard for no telling how long, until my eight-year-old foot trod upon it.

We fell into an immediate staring match, me and my newfound eye. I tried to pluck it out for a closer look. But it wasn't alone. It came attached to something skewered all the way through my instep. No blood, no pain, no pan-ic. Fascinated, I hippity-hopped around the side of the house to show Mama. She did not share my fascination but worry trumped her displeasure at me for breaking her hard and fast rule not to go barefoot before May.

Whew!

Poor Daddy couldn't look at it. The man had fought his way across Europe in World War II but fainted the previous year when Doctor Jordan put 167 stitches in my skinny leg. The result of a fateful game of Hide 'n Seek. I had slid in "home free" on top of two ham cans, the ra-zor-edged kind opened with a key, that Granddaddy used for watering his yard chickens. In a dreamlike state, transfixed by one of my pink ballerina shoes turning red, I hadn't immediately noticed the gashes down my shin. Uncle Tommy, our family risk-taker, swooped me up, declaring he'd had worse cuts on his eyeballs. He twisted a towel into a tourniquet to keep me from bleeding to death.

Whew!

That weirdly soothing eyeball remark came back to me as we confronted the one stuck in my foot. By the time Daddy drove me to our small-town hospital, his face had less color than his handkerchief. And there was Doc-tor Jordan again, the man who set the standard for hand-some, scowling over me. It was impossible to tell if the eye was attached to a wire he could simply pull straight out, or if it had barbs meant to hold it in a doll's head.

The good doctor pondered over snipping off the eyeball and pushing the metal out the top of my foot. Even as a child, a quite frightened child at that moment, I felt his angst. Dark eyebrows bunched in determination, he would get all set to pull it out and then shake his head and decide on pushing it. Over and over. I didn't dare look at Daddy, at least he hadn't hit the floor yet. Finally, in a magnificent leap of faith and courage, the doctor seized the eyeball with his tongs and yanked it out as smooth as you please.

Whew!

But it was also as rusty as you please. That meant a tetanus shot. Like Brother got when he was goofing off at the barn and stepped on a rusty nail. This would be my first. My wide-eyed expression when I saw the hypodermic needle made Doctor Jordan's lips thin into a straight line. He shook his head and tut-tutted about blue-eyed blondes being "the allergic type." Instead of the injection, he scratched the tip of the needle across my upper arm. It flushed beet red and sent the blood whooshing down my veins with such force I thought it would shoot out my fingertips. I watched in wonder as the doctor turned as pale as Daddy, and they both sat down.

Whew!

Over half a century later, I no longer have steadfast but weak-stomached Daddy, or jovial Uncle Tommy, or astute Doctor Jordan. Flashes of memory, however, that come along with these lovely little neuroma twinges remind me of how blessed I was to have grown up under their protection.

Chapter 4

A Mother's Touch is Forever

I paused before opening Mama's cedar chest, taking a moment to feel the polished wood as I had often seen her do, my hands tracing hers. And Daddy's. He'd cut down a red cedar in the side yard to make this chest for his new bride. Four children and seven grandchildren later, two decades past her death, Mama's prized possession was destined for my house, as Daddy was destined for Sister's house.

We had already gone through the contents of the chest. Divided the treasure, so to speak. Sister, Baby Sister, and I had spent an afternoon sitting on the plank floor where we had taken our first steps, examining memories we found slumbering amongst handmade quilts and embroidered pillowcases. Family photo albums filled with our smiling, and some not-so-smiling ancestors dredged up stories. We came across heart-pounding confessions tucked inside old letters, plus oddities like farm records detailing subsidies for growing kudzu. A silver purse that attended the premiere of *Gone With The Wind*, opera gloves, hatpins, coins, and a naked-lady lamp all gave us pause.

When I opened the chest again on moving day, I came across a nondescript wooden picture frame Sister had sandwiched between old linens.

"I didn't know if you'd want that or not," she said, glancing over my shoulder. "You made it, so I thought you should decide what to do with it."

"What in the world?" I pulled out the frame and turned it over. A quotation I had cross-stitched in a deep shade of purple—A Mother's Touch Is Forever—had faded to lavender in the sunbeams that brightened Mama's room during her long illness. Pretty hearts and flowers surrounding the words now denoted a pastel palette rather than the vibrant one I'd originally chosen. The fabric wore a definite vintage look.

Greeting it like an old friend, I closed my eyes and ran my fingers over the embroidery. Each stitch marked a moment in the lives of my own children. I was a working mom in those days, when they were six and twelve years old. We dragged this cross-stitched piece to piano lessons, Little League practices, doctor's visits, and play rehearsals.

Nowadays, whenever my son or daughter applauds my motherhood, I recognize the special touch of my mother, and the mothers of her generation, reaching through me and my friends to touch our children. We taught them to "rinse your hair until it squeaks" to "make your own sunshine on a rainy day" to "not be afraid of the biscuit dough" to "put on lipstick so you'll feel better" and "nothing cheers up a house like making the bed."

When Mama was peeved with Daddy, she'd grumble, "Don't do as I do, do as I say do," and warn us against marrying the baby of a family, or an only child. Like all youngsters, we were *hard of listening* because Sister and Baby Sister each married the baby of a family, and Brother and I both married only children.

Last fall my son said I'd taught him to "always do things in fours." As I disputed ever having said that, his happy grin made me realize, this was his way of announcing his wife was expecting Baby Number Four! Back in the 90s my husband teased me for buying fourteen miniature Christmas stockings to cross-stitch with our grand-babies' names and birthdates. Well, na-na-dee-boo-boo to him because this year I hung that last stocking on the mantel.

The day I beheld that old cross-stitch piece I'd given Mama, an image sprang to my mind from a visit to my daughter's home. Awakened in the wee hours of the morning by the crying of her new baby, I was making my way into the hall when I saw the sleep-deprived young mother slip into the nursery. The baby quieted instantly. Peering through the doorway, I'd received a wink from my daughter as she held her infant close and calmed her with a gentle touch.

I sat back on my heels and closed the chest. "You're right about this old cross-stitch, Sis. I know exactly what to do with it."

Chapter 5

Skating on the Septic Tank

On a recent trip back to my middle Georgia hometown, I found my Smith cousin, the eldest of my generation, standing with the aid of his cane in the town square. "I won all the races," he said, hugging me and speaking like he'd seen me last week instead of last year. Before I could ask what races, he gestured toward the busy intersection. "When I was young, they'd close both highways through town and let us boys roller-skate around the courthouse. With my short legs and low center of gravity, I won every race."

We stood a spell, imagining Cuz and his buddies skating dead heats around the Confederate Soldier statue.

His remembrance brought to mind my own skating "career." From the first time I'd watched the Winter Olympics on Auntie's TV, I dreamed of gliding around an ice rink. Unrealistic thoughts for a girl in the South, I turned my attention to a friend's Lock & Key roller skates. She lived in town and was blessed with a sidewalk, often skating all the way down to the drugstore. I'd sit on her front steps, almost too excited to breathe, clamping and tightening the metal contraptions onto the soles of my shoes. Maybe I wasn't mechanical enough, or my feet were too small, or my shoes were the wrong kind, but I never got past the corner before one of those skates came off. Pitifully skinned knees still come to mind whenever Melanie, a pop voice of my generation, sings, "*I Got a Brand-New Pair of Roller Skates.*"

The summer I turned twelve, a magnificent tent mushroomed on the edge of our little town. Special flooring went down, and voila! God had provided a roller rink. To afford boot skate rental, I did odd jobs for Auntie and saved up lunch money by taking sandwiches to school. On weekends, I begged rides to the rink. Sister obliged when she was home from the Atlanta Art Institute, or friends' parents took me along with their young skaters, or I'd spend the night with girlfriends in town. Gliding around that smooth oval, free as a bird. Faster and faster, frontward, backward, crossing arms and interweaving trajectories with schoolmates, all felt as easy as walking.

The rainbow of lights and booming Top Ten tunes drew young and old, skaters, daters, and spectators. I revolved amidst the hubbub inside the hazy bubble of neon, occasionally spotting Brother and Little Billy in the blur of the crowd. Several grades above me, they'd drop by between games at the pool hall to skate or girl-watch or check on me. I was fine, better than fine, my feet had wings!

The rollerblade inline skate generation will laugh, but sixty years ago, I pined for my very own pair of boot skates, high-top white leather with two sets of side-by-side wheels and rubber toe stops. By a miracle known as Santa-Mama, I got them. I must've tried them on and laced them up a hundred times between Christmas and the New Year. And then, you might say, the other skate dropped...

The fanciful tent, magic skating floor and all, packed up and left town. Worse than not having the rink, was having pristine new skates and nowhere to enjoy them. I canvassed the neighborhood for a place to skate. Not the highway, where riding my bike had already drawn the wrath of Mama; not Auntie's front walk, bordered by thorny rose bushes; not the pump island at Uncle's gas station, amid spraying gravel and honking horns.

One afternoon, as Baby Sister and I played house in the back yard, we swept leaves off the concrete slab Daddy had poured over our septic tank. I'd forgotten that, true to Mama's mantra of him—*anything worth doing is worth overdoing*—he'd used three times the amount of concrete necessary. My skates fell in love with that fair-sized, smooth-enough rectangle.

Crossing my feet at the corners, I skated dizzying circles around this personal rink. I didn't yet know my ability to skate on such a small surface had less to do with athletic prowess and more to do with inheriting short legs and a low center of gravity.

Chapter 6

Girls and Dolls

L ong ago when no one questioned whether or not girls should play with dolls, there were no "Barbies." My sisters and I were the closest things to "American Girls." We ate "Strawberry Shortcake" for dessert and found only cabbages in the "Cabbage Patch." In summer, we'd design outfits for Betsy McCall paper dolls and make twirly four o'clock blossom fairies. But with fall's arrival of the Sears Wishbook came the serious business of picking out our Christmas dolls. Leafing through the toy section and longing for pristine lace collars, tiny crinolines, and perfect little nylon socks worn with miniature Mary Janes, we could almost smell the sweet vanilla scent of vinyl skin. Every page of dolls was dog-eared as we each tried to choose one. The One.

Even in lean years, Santa-Mama managed to have our dolls under the tree on Christmas morning. Secretly using her old treadle sewing machine, she often made us dresses to match our dolls'. Her big failure came in 1947 when Sister wanted the "Sparkle Plenty" doll, based on the new baby born into the Dick Tracey comic strip. She turned out to be the hottest Christmas item of the year and sold out all over the country. Today I wish Mama could know about eBay and the vintage "Sparkle Plenty" now residing with Sister. Her long-awaited doll came complete with the original box and yellowed newspaper clipping about her scarcity.

Sister so adored her first doll, a life-size baby she named Babbie Lou, that seventy years later she still displays her head. This freaks out children of the *Chucky* movie era.

With our varying ages, Sister, Baby Sister, and I delighted over twenty years of doll evolution. We loved our baby dolls, Shirley Temple dolls, Revlon dolls, stand-alone dolls, and bride dolls. One year I got a ballerina my same height. She attached to my feet with elastic bands so I could dance with her. Some dolls blinked, some cried "Ma-Ma." When the trend turned more interactive, we consoled Tiny Tears and changed diapers for Betsy Wetsy.

Once I set my cap on a doll with a heartbeat. Brother

and Cousin Billy heard her ticking heart as a bomb and drafted her into their war games. Years later, I remembered Baby Heartbeat when I saw a behavioral study where girls were sent into a room containing a table of dolls. They talked for them, walked them around, and changed their wardrobes. Next, boys were sent in. They ignored the dolls and scanned the room for action toys. Seeing none, they grabbed up the dolls, pointed them at each other and made rat-a-tat gun noises.

A bride doll collector I know has three hundred beauties and still counting. My Barbie-loving friend finances her collection by refurbishing and reselling vintage Barbie outfits she finds online. Another friend, author of two successful mystery series, works out crime scenes with her dolls.

My daughter, foreshadowing her spiritual connection with creatures, preferred stuffed animals to dolls. Her little brother often gathered up her babies at night and tucked them in. His dad would rather see him put away his bike or hang up his ball glove, but our son was in training. He and his wife now have four live dolls, and he rarely misses bedtime snuggles.

The fall I was nine and sprawled on the porch perusing the Sears Wish Book, I wondered if I was too old for a doll. Then I turned the page and fell in love with beautiful Lotus Blossom, an Asian woman doll with dark, upswept hair and one rogue curl on her forehead. Along with an enigmatic expression, she wore pearl-drop earrings, a white silk tunic pantsuit, and sassy high heel sandals. Among the first dolls to have jointed elbows, knees, and ankles, my coming-of-age doll was posed on a stool with her legs crossed and one foot kicked up. In my bedroom today, she sits the same way and still makes me happy.

The January after Santa brought Lotus Blossom, Auntie threw a doll party for me. A dozen of my girlfriends came and brought their new dolls. We paraded them on a runway and selected as winner the stunning Queen Elizabeth Coronation Doll. The one faded picture I have of the doll party dispels a rumor going around that girls shouldn't be encouraged to play with dolls. Of the twelve smiling friends showing off their dolls that day, all became nurturing women who are also lawyers, judges, artists, realtors, educators, entrepreneurs, mathematicians, professors, bankers, and a writer—that one being me.

Chapter 7

Santa Rode a Mule

Did you haul out your favorite family story over the holidays? You know, funny or poignant depending upon your kin, the one that put a punctuation mark on the end of last year and energized you for the next. Mine is Mama's tale of her "Cud'n Henry" from Atlanta. Like most in 1929, her middle Georgia family was feeling the pinch of the nation's financial collapse, but that year's economic woes were compounded by her father's renal failure and loss of a kidney.

Listening to logs crackle in the fireplace and her mother's sweet soprano rendition of *Away in a Manger*, seven-year-old Sally—my mother—glued paper chains with her older siblings, Sue and Tommy. The aroma of fresh cedar filled their old farmhouse as they dressed the Christmas tree in every small bright object they could find. In the weeks approaching the holiday, Sally clung tenaciously to the myth of the jolly old man dropping down the chimney with presents. On Christmas Eve, however, she sat at the kitchen table trying to swallow her sweet potato supper along with Sue's revelation that they were not on Santa's list.

A sudden uproar from the dogs drew them to the kitchen door. From out in the freezing, drizzly night hailed a cheerful and familiar voice: "Merry Christmas! Merry Christmas!"

Sally peered past her father into the darkness and *what to her wondering eyes should appear* but her twelve-year-old cousin, Henry, all the way from Atlanta, perched atop a huge brown mule. A flickering kerosene lantern revealed the cold, determined lad hugging his short legs around the beast's middle. Gunny sacks bulging with Christmas gifts dangled from its sides.

Warming the boy with blankets and a hot supper, Sally's father learned how his sister in Atlanta had planned to surprise her country brother's family with gifts, but no one had been passing their way to bring them. She had waited too late to mail them, so her young son traveled seventy miles by bus, hitch-hiked another ten, and rode a borrowed mule the final four to play Santa. Too soon for Sally, he was off again to spend the night with other local relatives. Her cousin's small, pale face disappeared into the gloomy darkness as the mule clopped out of the yard and gained the muddy, deep-rutted road toward home—not exactly her image of *eight tiny reindeer,* but infinitely dearer. The lasting gift she received that year was a deeper understanding of Christmas, lovingly presented by the brave boy who gave up his holiday for hers.

Each year when we retell Mama's story, I am inspired by Cousin Henry's spunk. A late-in-life image of him from 1986 propels me forward into each coming year. Turning seventy and happily retired, he and his wife Ruth kicked back in their recliners and flipped on the news just in time to hear a reporter describing the person needed by the University of Georgia as interim president: a former leader of a major university, an energetic person willing to step into the breach, someone equally willing to step aside for the next administration. At that instant his phone rang. Dr. Henry King Stanford, President Emeritus of Miami University, was as far from his driving days then as he had been back when he was twelve, so he hopped a bus to Atlanta to meet with the regents. He would've ridden a mule if he'd had to.

Chapter 8

Good Bad-Words

Children get away with saying, singing, texting, and tweeting almost anything nowadays. At least once during every grandchild's visit, I cover my ears and exclaim, "Grandmother on board, clean up the language please!"

Back when I was a teen, Mama wouldn't even let me get away with calling Brother a fool. She plunked me down at the kitchen table with the Bible and made me memorize Matthew 5:22: "…whoever is angry with his brother…whoever says, 'You fool!' will be in danger of hell fire."

In fourth grade, I'd had a prior kitchen table session with Mama, along with a jumbo box of Crayolas. She had

been in earshot that day when I got off the school bus re-
peating the "N" word. I understood it as the name of a
color until she had me read aloud the names of all sixty-
four crayons. And then she explained why that word was
not to be found in my vocabulary either.

My mother was known to grumble "Hector Protec-
tor" if she became aggravated while sewing. And on oc-
casion "Damnation and every other kind of nation" waft-
ed out of her kitchen on the stench of burnt biscuits. Daddy's strongest disparaging remark was "Son-of-a-gun."
Happily, I had an uncle with the fitting nickname, Bull.
Hailing from "Nashville-*damn*-Tennessee" he was a *hell-
uva* education for this small-town Baptist girl. Uncle
Bull's favorite adjective was the Lord's name, which he
took in vain as regularly as breaths of fresh air. Irreverent
and side-splitting silly, he seasoned his verbiage with
damns and hells and bellowed outlandish expletives
about nothing more serious than misplaced car keys.
Even when I didn't know what he meant, his belly laughs
and Auntie's scolding told me he was being naughty.

Good-humoredly cussing and fussing, Uncle Bull
was an endless source of fascination. I spent joyful weekends sailing through the countryside with him, wallowing
untethered on the bench seat of his big Ford Galaxy, dis-
tinctive not only for its unusual shade of baby blue, but
from the obvious brushstrokes Uncle Bull left when he
took a notion to paint it. He encouraged me to roll down
the windows and stick out my damn arms, and even my

fool head, freeing me to test air resistance and my parental boundaries. Our jaunts usually brought us to someone's house where an appliance needed repair— refrigerator, washer, iron, oven. When offered payment, my uncle would give me a conspiratorial wink, and shout, "Hell no, we just came by for a damn visit."

Good bad-words were plentiful and colorful whenever Auntie called upon him to crawl under their house to rescue a litter of kittens. About the size and shape of Ralph Kramden in *The Honeymooners*, he would roar oaths that roughly translated, "To the moon, Alice."

My parents kept Uncle Bull neutralized pretty well, but his mischief was as unpredictable as the path of a tornado. He touched down on our porch the afternoon Daddy had assembled Sister, Brother, Baby Sister, and me for the naming of our new calf. We each wrote our choice on a slip of notebook paper, folded it twice, and ceremoniously dropped it into Grandma's churn. Baby Sister was poised to draw the name and hand it to Daddy when Uncle Bull bounded up and added one of his choosing. Daddy unfolded the slip of paper Baby Sister pulled out, stared solemnly at it, and then said in his most terse tone of voice, "Draw again." Fifty years later we are still laughing about how Curly Top the calf should have been called Hockey Roses.

I couldn't deny that Mama had God firmly on her side when it came to the word fool. For a while I disguised it as foolish, but she caught on. After that, I resorted to hissing at Brother, "You old...*ISH* thing." Tame by today's standards, at least it was clever. But not clever enough for me to dodge Mama's peach-tree switch. Although I am not allowed to say the actual word, let me assure you my Mama was nobody's...*ISH* thing.

Chapter 9

Million Dollar Max

In 1964, Uncle Sonny gave my grandmother a dog named Maximillion *doo-doddy-doo*, some foreign name she couldn't pronounce. Sonny expounded on how much he'd paid for a real German police dog, and even more for getting him trained to protect Nanny.

"Lord have mercy, protect me from what?" Nanny wanted to know.

She shortened the dog's name to Max and made a pet out of him. He slept with his chin on her bedroom slippers at night, rolled in the four o'clock blooms when she hung out clothes, and sniffed out snakes so she could pick blackberries. He took snake sniffing seriously and kept a pace or two in front of her when she walked down the railroad spur that ran between her house and ours. Nanny baked cheese biscuits for her new companion and found some of the pounds she'd lost after Granddaddy died.

The only other pet she had that wasn't destined for a stew pot was another uncle's Amazon parrot named Doc. Big as a turkey buzzard with feathers in all the primary colors, Doc could crack black walnuts with the can opener on the end of his face. He could say anything he took a notion to, but ever since he waltzed out of his cage and climbed to the top of the peach tree in Nanny's back yard, he mostly repeated her, "Lo-o-o-rd have mercy!"

One Saturday, Doc was in his cage catching the breeze through the propped open window while Nanny and I shelled peas. Sonny's convertible coasted into the shade of a red cedar in the front yard. Max set his tail at a jaunty angle and arced gracefully off the porch. Big and deep-chested, thick fur glistening, he loped across the yard with what even I recognized as athletic certitude. He gave Sonny's hand a welcoming lick, and Sonny yelled, "Mama, this is a *guard* dog, not a *lap* dog!"

"He's *my* dog," Nanny said. Max flumped down at her feet and rested his muzzle on saucer-sized forepaws. "And he suits me just fine."

The black shepherd's neat tan brow rose and fell with the tone of his mistress's voice.

"You're living in another world down here," Sonny groused. "This is the sixties. You ought to see what's going on in Atlanta. Hippies sleeping in the street in front of my restaurant, smoking pot all the way to Virginia Highlands."

"I thought hippies were just wanting peace," Nanny said, hefting herself out of the low chair. "We ain't studying him, are we Max A. Million? Let's go find a pot of our own for these butter beans. She flounced into the house with Max half a flounce behind.

"Do you have to call him that?"

"That's his name, ain't it?"

"Lo-o-rd have mercy," moaned Doc, the parrot.

Sonny rolled his eyes, peeling cellophane off a fresh pack of Winston's. "If she knew what he cost, she'd be calling him Million Dollar Max."

After supper, Sonny came out on the back porch. Baby Sister was practicing how to tie bow ribbons in Max's fur, and I was polishing his toenails in Avon's Congo Red.

Sonny choked on a mouthful of smoke. "What on earth are y'all doing?"

"Playing dress-up with Max A. Million," we chimed. "Nanny said it was okay."

The dog positioned his ears at nine o'clock and lolled out his tongue, a shade of pink that closely matched the ribbons decorating his dark fur.

Sonny exploded. "It's not okay with me! Get that stuff off him right this minute." His cigarette landed in the canna lilies, and he flew back in the house. "Mama!

I'm taking that dog back to Atlanta for more training, whether you like it or not."

Nanny did not like it. She wouldn't come outside the next morning when they drove off. Max sat up high on the back seat of the convertible like a politician riding down Jefferson Avenue in the Dairy Festival parade. He was sitting the same way when Sonny brought him back the next afternoon.

"You win, Mama," was all Sonny said.

It took some doing, but we finally got the story out of him. Seems they'd been sailing down Peachtree Street when they caught the light at Ponce de Leon. Sonny was figuring what another round of training was going to cost and didn't notice another convertible pull up in the next lane. As the light changed, bloodcurdling screams came from the woman driver of the second convertible. Hysterical, she had her eyes glued on the rearview mirror full of German Police dog riding in her back seat. She couldn't see his happy eyes and thumping tail past his inch-long canines. Sonny gave up on Max being a guard dog right then and there.

Nanny was happy to have her companion back and soon proved she didn't need him for protection. Amid hosting a wedding shower, she glanced out the window and saw Cousin Billy, who stayed with her when he was home from college, stumbling across her front yard in front of a deputy holding a pistol.

"Nanny!" Billy bawled, "Nanny, come tell him who I am!" Hitchhiking to town, like he'd done a thousand times before, Billy had been mistaken for an escapee from the nearby reform school.

Nanny barreled out of her house, swooped down the front steps, and jumped in between gun and grandson before we could blink.

"You know this boy, Mrs. Callaway?" the deputy was stupid enough to ask.

Nanny shooed Billy safely onto the porch and turned on the man. "I'll tell you what I know—I'm looking at a man who's lost his job as soon as I get in the house and call the sheriff."

"Good God, Mama," Sonny said when heard about that stunt. "Where was Max."

"Asleep under the spirea," she said. "No need to bother him."

Three years later, Nanny fell seriously ill. She and Max went to live in Atlanta with Sonny and his wife, Carol. Caring for Nanny, Carol became attached to the big dog. The feeling was mutual and when Nanny died, Max shifted his allegiance to Carol.

A flower child of the '60s with corn silk hair, Carol took him to her boutique to keep Sonny from worrying about her working down on lower Peachtree Street.

"I don't know why she has to have a shop down in the Tight Squeeze district," he told Mama, "but a loafer the size of Max will make somebody think twice about bothering her. If he doesn't scare off the customers."

With her patient smile, Carol said, "To sell trendy clothes, I have to be with the people who wear them. My clients will love Max. He's a lady's man."

Max breezed to and from the shop with Carol and claimed the middle dressing room. Snoozing on a velvet bench behind lavender chintz curtains, he never deterred a single hip-hugging, bell-bottomed sale. Even as her block fell into disrepair, free-spirited Carol prospered and felt safe. One summer evening, she was counting the day's receipts when a man waving a pistol barged in off the street.

"Get out here and lay down," he snarled. "Get down on the floor!"

A scream locked in Carol's throat as she darted a desperate glance at the dressing room. The robber began to curse, so she got down and crawled into the middle of the sales floor.

He pointed the gun directly at her. "Raise your head, and I'll put a hole in it, bitch."

Carol buried her face in the rug, sucking in the raw smell of burlap. Silently she summoned her dog, but he was oblivious to her telepathic commands. She felt stupid for her false sense of security.

The man emptied the cash register and scrabbled under the counter for her back-up cash. He ripped the phone cord out of the wall and flung paisley and tie-dyed clothing across the room.

Hearing him stumble toward the door, Carol prayed he'd leave without hurting her. The bully hesitated, turned, and stalked over to her. Hauling back his foot, he kicked her across the room into the base of the sales counter.

Through her pain, Carol almost missed the awe-inspiring sight of her German police guard dog in full-blown personal defense mode. Max launched off his tufted perch and rocketed through the air wearing a cape of lavender chintz, curtain rod and all. He body-slammed Carol's attacker and bore him backward through the plate glass window into the middle of Peachtree Street. Carol heard the man's garbled shrieks and learned it took eight grown men to pull her super hero off him.

The following year, it was with great confidence that Sonny and Carol watched a change come over their dog. Million Dollar Max abandoned his chosen fitting room and spent his days hulking in the corner of the boutique beside their new baby's bassinette. Head on forepaws, his sandy brow rose and fell with the tone of his tiny mistress's coos.

Chapter 10

I'm Here

When teachers called role at school, I never quite reached the level of sophistication to answer, "Present." Overcome with childhood insecurity, I was stuck mumbling, "Here." Throughout my life, people have demonstrated to me that *here* is about the best place one can be.

"I'm here."

When I was in my twenties, a new neighbor turned those words into a challenge as she stood on my doorstep with her vacuum cleaner and assorted cleaning supplies. I shook my head, embarrassed to let an acquaintance clean my neglected house. "Don't insult me by refusing again." She bustled past me and went to work. I couldn't have summoned the strength to insult a fly; I was pregnant and suddenly very grateful *here* is where this generous woman wanted to be.

A decade later, to spare my children moving their possessions from our country-club home to my post-divorce condo, I determined to accomplish the job while they were at school. I was physically and emotionally spent by the time the quiet, dignified owner of the moving company showed up with lunch for his workers.

"Here," he said, handing me a chilidog from The Varsity and unwrapping one for himself.

As we sat on the concrete steps in the breezeway to my little flat, chowing down on chilidogs and onion rings, I considered the reality he had unknowingly spoken. *Here* was my new home. In that moment, what had seemed like the end of my world started to feel like a beginning.

Who doesn't love arriving at family get-togethers and being heralded by children shouting, "She's here!"

I am not the best cook in the bunch, not by a long shot, so there is no way my covered dish generated their excitement. I eagerly joined in their chorus as the next loved one arrived. When that person turned out to be my aging father, someone invariably asked him, "How are you feeling?"

He'd perk up and answer, "I'm here."

I wonder if he knew how much our family counted on him being exactly that. How much I counted on being able to drive into his yard and leap onto his welcoming porch with my standard, "Yoo-hoo, Daddy, I'm here."

Now he isn't around anymore to sit and patiently listen to my little diatribes on life, but I share them anyway, confident he is still *here* in spirit.

A co-worker's actions spoke the word *here* louder than his voice ever could have, the weekend my teenager ran away from home. Wordlessly willing the phone to ring, he sat *here* with me, hour after hour, day after day. He did not know me well but he knew a parent's heart.

Another time, an offhanded comment that I couldn't really afford to go out to lunch with an old friend, brought her to my door with her checkbook. Already providing for a family of five, she was still willing to say, "I'm here."

I won't recount the times that same gal-pal appeared with a bottle of Zinfandel and a bag of Doritos. We said a lot more than *here* on those nights! But the message was the same.

And now a new year is *here*. With its unbelievably futuristic number, this year loomed up and announced itself. Bestowing the joy of a granddaughter's wedding and the promise of spring, it also holds the global specters of illness, tragedy, and need. I have almost reached that time of life Rose Kennedy spoke of when she said her job was "to show up and smile."

But I am no longer interested in being sophisticated. I do not want to be merely present. I want to raise my hand high, maybe wave it around a bit, and declare, "I'm here!"

Chapter 11

The Wedding Gift

I was kidnapped on my wedding day. The perpetrator drove boldly up the driveway and strode through the house, issuing commands. Daddy almost saluted when ordered to place my billowing gown on the back seat of her car. The creamy white bun askew on the back of her head shone like a beacon in the prenuptial storm. Mama handed me over without a whimper.

Aunt Tee, the usually mild-mannered wife of Daddy's brother, was formidable when she snatched a bride. Her sky blue eyes, luminous behind thick bifocals, meant business. I'd expected to leave home that afternoon carefully coifed and prettily put together in bridal regalia, not spirited away before breakfast in sponge rollers and Brother's cut-off jeans.

This bride-napper drove silently to the church where I was to be married and guided me into a delicate pink, lavender-scented room. Months of wedding jitters and angst over last-minute calamities evaporated. The relief was as delicious as the brunch set out on the tea table. Suddenly the day was not about the wedding. It was about the bride. It was about me!

Devoted to her mission of dressing brides since her first niece married in 1958, my aunt lost count of the women she ministered to in this special way. A plaque honors her in the bride's room of her church, but she smoothed veils and nerves all over the state.

The day of my wedding she didn't come armed with platitudes or advice on achieving a long and happy marriage like hers. She brought her innate story-telling talent. As she gave my cumbersome gown a final lick with the iron, I polished my toenails and heard again how Grandma had vowed not to love me.

"I can see her now," Aunt Tee chuckled. "She was miffed to find out your mother was expecting. Thought your Daddy couldn't afford another baby."

"What changed her mind?" I asked, knowing full well.

"You! You were the cutest, sweetest, fattest little thing in the world. And it was sweltering hot the summer you were born. One afternoon your Mama missed you from your bassinet. Grandma had you out on the porch in a foot tub, cooling you off with a sponge bath."

"My only real memory of Grandma is her biscuits."

"She'd be proud of that." Aunt Tee scrutinized my veil for an errant wrinkle. "Only spanking she gave your Daddy was for feeding her biscuits to the dog."

At the moment of greatest decision in my young life, I was uplifted by the certainty that family transcends change. Laughing over old stories, I glimpsed the future through the lens of the past.

"What kind of dress did you wear when you married?"

She slid my going-away skirt onto the ironing board. "It was this same pretty shade of blue. A suit I wore home on the train that morning from Atlanta. I'd gone to see about my sister who was sick and I was late getting back. The preacher gave up on me getting married that day, but I fooled him. I made it home right as he was leaving."

As she deftly rehung my skirt and turned her attention to the jacket, I took a barefoot stroll through the building, letting my nail polish dry. My aunt bestowed upon me that which she hadn't had. It had nothing to do with the cavernous church or the beaded dress. Her gift was time. Unhurried and unharried, I wandered the corridors to the sanctuary. Roses and magnolias were banked exactly as I had envisioned around the altar where I'd been christened. With their beauty, I inhaled the wonder

and promise of life. My life. Cloistered in peace and quiet, I reflected on those who loved me and their good
wishes for my future. Like the biblical Mary, *I treasured
up all these things and pondered them in my heart.*

The first strains of the Wedding March found Aunt
Tee tucking an embroidered hanky under my bouquet and
ripping a price tag off the elbow of Daddy's new suit. Her
dear face doesn't appear in one wedding picture. During
the ceremony, she was gathering all my paraphernalia;
during the reception, she was organizing my traveling
clothes; during the chaotic rice pelting scene, she was
taking charge of my bridal gown and veil.

No, you don't see her in the wedding album. But I
do.

Section II

I am part of all I have met.
Tennyson's Ulysses

Chapter 12

A Bolt in the Blue

I didn't especially want to take flying lessons, but with a husband who insisted on learning and two precious babies in the sky with us, I *very much* wanted to know how to land. Maybe because I had a lifelong penchant of going the wrong way—in the out, up the down, and struggling with boxes rather than "open other end."

"Passive aggressive," my cousin said.

As the lone female in my 1974 ground school class, I tolerated considerable posturing from male counterparts. Each man showed up the day I soloed, armed with scissors for the tradition of cutting off a new pilot's shirt. Thankfully, I'd had the foresight to wear two shirts.

One cold February morning during my preflight in-
spection, a close visual check of the plane's exterior, I
blew an insect out of the pitot tube, lest it impede the stall
alarm. As I wiped off frost to check the oil, I realized the
cotter pin that shut the oil door flap was missing. Without
thinking twice, I used a bobby pin. If anything, it held the
flap tighter than the cotter pin. It elevated me to a new
level of respect, though, because the next burly man to
preflight that plane found my bobby pin and dared not
take it up.

Just over five feet tall, I knew from my first attempt
that I couldn't see in front of the plane when I pulled up
the nose and flared for landing. I learned to gauge distance from the runway by looking out the side window. I
never bounced a landing that way, not one, while my tes-
tosterone-filled colleagues routinely plowed into the tar-
mac. I finished practice one afternoon to find eleven dis-
gruntled men lined up against the fence with their instructor shouting, "See, *that's* how you do it!"

I suppressed a smile until I had taxied past them.

My crusty flight instructor, Mac, adjusted teaching
like I did learning. He had me flying over the Talledega
Racetrack, vacant in winter, when he reached over and
pulled the power. I was forced to learn how to "slip" the
plane onto the infield for a touch-and-go. Quite fun and
illegal.

As my licensing exam approached, I flew an ap-
proved cross-country course from my home field in cen-

tral Alabama, round-trip to Huntsville via Fort Payne. Three, one-hundred-mile, legs. I was cautioned not to wander over the Redstone Arsenal outside Huntsville. Cold War Era military was touchy about atomic research areas. "Shoot you out of the sky," Mac warned before stubbing out his cigar and nodding off in the co-pilot seat.

As I approached Fort Payne and centered over its beacon, the tachometer needle danced from one extremity of the dial to the other. I shook Mac awake. "Why's the tach doing that?"

"I dunno." He yawned, and went back to sleep.

I flew on.

Coming within range, I radioed Huntsville Tower. A lazy drawl vectored me around the arsenal and reported a navy jet in the pattern ahead. An edge of disdain in the voice indicated the controller wondered why I was in his airspace and not home fixing supper. I dialed in his coordinates and banked into my first turn. As quick and sure as if it were powered by rubber band, the plane broke! Its nose jerked up and then slammed back down clouding the cockpit with cigar ash. The Cessna 150 bucked like a deranged bronco, smashing my teeth together so hard they felt shattered.

I screamed, "Mac! What's happening?"

He gripped his seat cushion and gave me a blank stare.

"Wh—what do I do?"

"Pray," he gasped, "if you believe in that sort of

thing." Then he burst into tears. The seasoned retiree who'd logged thousands of hours had never experienced an equipment failure.

I grabbed the mic, now dislodged and snaking around the cabin. "Huntsville T—Tower, this is Cessna Six-Zero-One-Zero-Golf. We have a prob—problem"

"Well, ma'am, you're not DEE-claring an EE-mergency are you?"

Wrestling with the column, I yelled, *"Yes! I declare an emergency!"*

The controller snapped on a different persona. "Copy, Cessna 6010-Golf." He gave me a straight-in heading directly over the arsenal, adding crisply, "I'm moving the jet."

Irrationally wondering how much that would cost the navy, I caught glimpses of the airport when the nose of the plane bucked low.

"Three miles out, altitude eighteen," the controller advised. "Crop-duster strip east a quarter mile." I couldn't locate it, and Mac was sobbing into his hands. After a pause, the controller added, "Don't put down in a field, ma'am, they're marshy from rain. We've got some big parking lots."

Our designated runway beckoned, but its leading edge dropped off sharply. If we were short, we were dead. I glued my eyes on the call numbers painted near the end, the ones meant to be overflown before touch-down. As Cessna 6010G gulped her last foot of altitude, I held my breath, looked out the left window, and settled her onto the pavement—barely—before ever reaching the big white numbers. The world went so still it was disorienting. Covered head to toe with hives, I planted my feet on solid ground. *Thank you, God.*

Mac slammed his door so hard the cockpit rocked. "I knew redheads were bad luck," he growled, chomped a cigar, and stalked away.

The mechanics who towed the plane said I should have switched off the engine—*the last* thing I'd have done. "Rocker arm boss assembly in your number two cylinder broke into eight pieces," they explained. "Shook every bolt 'cept one out of your engine mount." Without weight in front, we would have fallen tail down. *Thank you, God!*

I never flew with Mac again. But I had learned to land.

Chapter 13

The Dream

Last night I dreamed of Lindsey Scott. It was 1980 again, and we were in Jacksonville for college football's Southeastern Conference Georgia/Florida game.

He, in a white Number 24 jersey, stood in the backfield and raised his hand overhead to wave at me in the stands. I, wife of a die-hard Georgia fan, was easy to spot in a red jumpsuit resembling the fireplug doghouse of our mascot, Uga III. Before I could return the young athlete's wave, a football slammed into his hand, and he proceeded to make the sweetest run in SEC history.

Why would I dream such a thing? If you had asked, I would have said I didn't have a football story.

I had spent fifteen years of home games with UGA's Sanford Stadium fifty-yard line running up my skirt-tail, but that was short tenure by true fan standards. Those games were as much a test of my endurance as the team's. I committed tailgate recipes to memory, held babysitter numbers as close to the vest as secret plays, and ran options all week on how to most efficiently get us to kickoff. I envied the players not having the additional burden of shopping for what to wear. Did you know that ladies in a bathroom will break in line and come to blows rather than get behind a red jumpsuit with gazillion buttons?

I don't know if the football phenomenon in Athens is due to a natural homing instinct, or if UGA switches on some sort of magnetic field "between the hedges." There is paint that makes entire walls magnetic, so it occurs to me that the same technology could be in place in the beer industry, attracting unwitting alumni. Before my family figured out an actual excuse to move back to Georgia, we joined that annual exodus. We've been known to drive hundreds of miles, fly in from other states, and even come by boat across Lake Hartwell. A couple of friends would have crawled if they'd had to.

My football seasons were happy blurs of friends, fashion, and food. At least that's how it was until my defining moment with Lindsey Scott. Reality was a little different from my dream, though. A gaggle of us went to the 1980 Gatorbowl via a golfing trip to St. Simons. In the last minute of the game, down 21 to 20, we were tired and discouraged. Around me, fidgety fans groped for the punch lines of old jokes, rehashed rounds of golf, mixed covert drinks, and wrestled with stadium seats.

Being preoccupied myself with that age-old question of which is uglier, a bulldog or a gator, I panned down field just as Buck Belue let fly his golden pass. My gaze settled on Lindsey Scott the instant he reached for it.

I stood up.

Number 24 tucked the ball and ducked his head.

"Hey," I said, my eyes glued on the runner. I wind-milled my arms. "Hey, you guys. *Look!*"

By the time our man had gobbled up the ninety-three yards to the end zone, 70,000 seats had emptied, their occupants airborne with Georgia victory or Florida defeat. Larry Munson had broken his chair and taped his legendary broadcast with Loran Smith. Drinks were spilled, backs pounded, and goalposts demolished. Fans on both sides screamed hysterically, "Did you see that?"

Most people have watched the replay so often since, they're convinced they actually did.

Athens is still my home, but now I run cross-grain to the football culture. It's hard to see professors blocked from parking lots, students locked out of libraries, and the real business of education come a distant second. I must admit, though, in fall when the Dogs meet the Gators, I whip up tailgate fare, settle in front of my television, and dream of Lindsey Scott.

Chapter 14

The Egg and I

With five words, Baby Sister struck fear in my heart: "You bring the deviled eggs."

As host of our family Easter shindig, she was within her rights to assign my covered dish. But, oh Lord, despite my best efforts, my eggs will look like they were peeled with a weed whacker.

Aiming to raise my game, I went shopping for a product I'd seen on TV—egg-shaped plastic containers that promised to turn out eggs as smooth as those Auntie specialized in. Six months short of a hundred years young, Auntie glared over the top of her bifocals at a preacher who mentioned cholesterol in proximity to her deviled eggs. She informed him, "Not a single deviled egg has ever walked out of this Baptist church."

Don't get me wrong, my ugly eggs are delicious. I tweaked Auntie's recipe with a tip from a friend in Atlanta who happens to be a renowned chef. A Georgia governor once made a fool of himself by eating an entire tray of her deviled eggs at a statehouse reception.

My problem is presentation. Over the years I've heeded the advice of experienced devilers: use fresh eggs, don't use fresh eggs; cover them with cold water, drop them into boiling water; add vinegar, add baking soda; cover the pot, don't cover the pot; time precisely, cool completely; shake boiled eggs in a glass jar to break the shell, roll boiled eggs across counter with your palm to crack the shells. Talk about walking on eggshells! I've tried it all, even an online tip for baking rather than boiling. Baked eggs turn out okay, but they are so rubbery they bounce.

I admit to being a fraud during my children's school years. Whenever they were assigned to bring deviled eggs to a function, I'd swing by Mr. Thrasher's general store on my way home from work and pick up a tray of his magnificent double-yolks. I'd be legging it over there right now if he was still around.

Maybe my conflict with eggs is a holdover from childhood. I was also inept at finding Easter eggs. So much so, my Sunday School teacher created a "Found the Least" category and awarded me a baby chick. In those "olden days," Easter chicks were dyed in bright colors and mine was red. Ergo his name, but I should have called him Lazarus. One chilly spring morning, I found my new biddy dead on the porch, his spiky orange feet kicked straight up. Mama wrapped him in a towel and tucked him in the warm oven. Before long we heard him peeping. Red grew into a handsome pet rooster who never again saw the inside of an oven.

My grocery store delighted me by selling the magic egg-cookers. It was the same box I'd seen on TV picturing a dozen perfect eggs. Hurrying home, I opened the box and lost some delight. Only half a dozen plastic cookers rolled out. Also, the assembly process was more involved than I'd expected. Each had four parts plus detailed oiling instructions for releasing perfectly cooked eggs. While I was fiddling with them, I threw the remaining six eggs into a pot with six others I was boiling for potato salad.

Eventually, I got the contraptions I'd bought filled with yolks and whites, and floating upright in boiling water like bobbers on a fishing line. I eyed them with fascination for the prescribed fifteen minutes, while peeling potato salad eggs. As soon as the timer went off, I dipped them out and carefully followed the disassembly instructions. All six eggs turned out the same—sunk into the bottom half of their plastic shells and dimpled as golf balls. Drat!

I vowed—again—never to waste money—again—on something I'd seen on TV.

Turning to toss the oily, unacceptable half-eggs in with those I'd peeled for potato salad, I found myself staring at twelve silky smooth ovoids already in the pot. Not a single divot. I couldn't tell you how much water I put them in, how long they'd boiled or cooled, or how I'd gone about peeling them. But there they were. Flawless!

I vowed—again—never to stress over deviled eggs. Good thing, because my Easter gift from Baby Sister was a fancy Snap 'N Lock double-decker deviled egg carrier.

Chapter 15

Tree Hugging

I don't think of myself as a "tree hugger" but Theodosia Garrison's words speak to me:

The kindliest thing God ever made,
His hand of very healing laid,
Upon the fevered world is shade.

Triple that for summers in Georgia. My sister-in-law's reaction on her first visit here was to hitch up her shoulders to her ears and exclaim, "The trees are so close!" In North Dakota where she lived, most trees march out across the plains as wind breaks for distant fields. We Southerners like our trees right on the doorstep. We encourage them to brush our byways, drape their leafy boughs across our highways, and bestow upon us their blessed shade. Fly into Atlanta and take note of all the lush, welcoming green.

Despite the beauty and positive environmental impact of trees, we decimate them. Bulldozed for construction and mutilated for power lines, they are generally taken for granted. Nothing tries harder. They clothe, and feed, and shelter us. Trees endure, often here when we come into this world and still here when we leave.

Long before I came to Athens, Georgia, with its renowned *Tree That Owns Itself*, I understood the love that compels one to protect a tree. The landscape of my middle Georgia childhood had changed with the death of the century oak that cooled the farmhouse where I was raised. Its towering head could be seen six miles away, and I was painfully aware of its demise as soon as I drove through town and turned toward home. I'd whiled away youthful afternoons in the plank swing suspended from one of its massive limbs. Drawing circles in the red dirt with my bare toes inevitably twisted the swing's long ropes, so I'd lift my feet and lean back, whirling dizzily with my eyes fixed on three dilapidated boards so far aloft as to be almost out of sight—Daddy's tree-fort from the summer he was seven. Symbols of my own roots.

Fearfully, what goes up must come down, especially in Georgia's weather extremes. I have a Scarlet Oak in my yard with the capacity to wipe out my house, and one afternoon a pine fell beside my mailbox less than a minute after I'd posted a letter. I like to envision God holding up his hand, saying, "Wait...wait...okay she's gone, *drop* the tree!"

Of course, we eventually lose even our special trees. My sister's Victorian home has more light since the city removed a gnarly, diseased old oak from the right of way. But those left who knew it as The Prayer Oak mourn its passing. Back in the 1920s, that silent sentinel witnessed a miracle outside the sickroom of a dying girl. Her classmates flocked to the tree—a hale and hearty specimen in those days—and spent the night in earnest prayer beneath its boughs. At daybreak, their revived friend opened her window and waved.

My brother-in-law insisted I walk the acreage I'd inherited from my father. Offering me his snake guards, plus an afternoon of his time, he took me and my son in search of corner pins. I'd expected the briars and scrub pine we navigated—me robot-walking in hard plastic, thigh-high snake guards—but deep within the property, where I wouldn't have otherwise ventured, we came upon the remnant of a stand of forest giants. That's what trees do, they stand. Tall. Proud. Thanks to my loving and persistent brother-in-law for that moment of recognition—*my* trees on *my* land from *my* family.

Do you know that trees communicate with one another? When one comes under heavy attack by insects, it emits pheromones alerting nearby relatives to mobilize chemical defenses stored in their trunks. These wonders deserve to be celebrated, as they are all over the world, in religion, folklore, and art. Jesus prayed beneath an olive tree and Buddha was enlightened under a Bodhi tree. I may borrow from African tradition and make a bottle tree. Not to capture evil spirits but to enjoy the sun and wind playing with colorful up-ended glass bottles. I applaud Yoko Ono's idea of installing Wish Trees in her art exhibits. Since 1981, untold thousands of wishes have been written down and tied onto the limbs of her trees. '*Imagine*' John Lennon smiling.

Oh, come on, let's go out and hug a tree—you know you want to.

Chapter 16

Is God a Border Collie?

Dogs scare me to death. It's not their fault I had a skirmish with one of their kind when I was at an impressionable age, but a mere bark throws me into a cold sweat. I consulted a dog-behavior expert about my irrational fear, explaining how uncertain I am of their territorial limits and sensitive spots, plus my complete inability to differentiate between curious canines and curs. Unhelpfully, the professor responded, "I don't find that irrational at all."

My family advised me to raise a big dog as therapy, so I adopted a white German shepherd-timberwolf puppy. To instill a sweet nature from the get-go, I named him Cookie. I took him for obedience training right away, but he had already maxed out on size for the puppy class. We took the adult class, where Cookie mostly learned how to make me obey him.

Imagine my embarrassment when our son's Chow evicted me from his house where I was baby-sitting a grandchild. Not knowing the dog's way of asking for a treat was to chomp his teeth at you, dog-phobic me misinterpreted that to the nth degree.

Recently someone sent around an email about respecting the space of dogs wearing yellow ribbons. Yellow signifies they may be in training, have health issues, or be scared or reactive. Since I am both scared and reactive, can I wear a yellow ribbon and get the same respect?

Before I go to someone's house, I *always* ask if they have a dog. If so, how friendly? Dog owners don't intentionally lie, but they view their dogs through a loving lens. A man who asked me to stop by and notarize a document for him said, "Oh, I have a couple of puppies out back in a fence." I rang his bell and came face to snout with two adult Doberman Pinschers barking and snarling through his front window.

I screamed, "Don't open the door!"

Their master put them in the back yard—where they promptly ran through an open gate, around the side of the house, and straight at me. No court will ever accept as mine the shaky signature I scribbled that day.

Conversely, I wasted a day's worth of serotonin the first time I went to play Mah Jongg at a new friend's house. She mentioned having a small dog, but a sign posted in her driveway said—*Parking for Danes Only*. Small dog, my foot! Ever grateful for a cell phone, I called the hostess again. From out in her yard, I could hear the lady from *Denmark*, who owned a tiny poodle, laughing her head off.

A recipe swap at church turned into angst over taking goodies to shut-ins, until I decided to make my deliveries at an assisted living home. Ensconced in that safe environment, maybe I felt too virtuous approaching the first recipient's door. My knock was greeted by vicious-sounding, hinge-rattling barks. Fleeing to the lobby with my heart in my throat, I whimpered, "Okay! I get it, God. You have the power to put a dog anywhere you want."

That lesson was soon repeated on a simple errand to recycle magazines. After opening my front car door, I realized I could hurt my back hoisting heavy bags over the driver's seat. I pulled open the back door and filled the rear seat instead. Sensing a presence, I looked down and locked eyes with a pit bull. Frozen to the marrow, I could not determine if she "be friend or foe." Her inscrutable expression never wavered. Employing my purse as a shield between tooth and shin, I crawled inside the car on top of the magazines. I eventually got up the nerve to inch my hand past the dog's maw and ease the rear door closed. Unperturbed, the beast stepped to the front door I had left open and *got in the driver's seat*.

Huddled in my own back seat with a pit bull chauffeur, I was too stunned to pray. I suddenly started laughing. I remembered a fellow writer saying, "Most people think of God as a shepherd, but He's really a border collie." I laughed harder imagining God herding me into these ludicrous situations with dogs. I can't say this pit bull completely mended the blow made to my psyche long ago, but as she turned to look at me from the front seat, she smiled.

Okay, maybe not, but she wagged her short tail and didn't bark.

Chapter 17

Beach Vacation '61

When my big sister, an artist, announced she was painting a portrait of me, one of me holding a monkey, all I could force myself to say was, "That's great." Even though I didn't think so.

My husband's career, not mine, revolves around nonhuman primates. Sister had already painted *Smith Farm*, an award-winning landscape of our family home-place, for Brother, and she'd given *Sally's Room*, a cherished still-life of our mother's bedroom, to Baby Sister. Now it was my turn, but…me with a monkey? Really?

A few months later, since my hubby had gone monkey-watching in a Costa Rican cloud forest, I called upon Sister to take me for an out-patient procedure. She was at my bedside when the anesthesiologist administered my first dose of "happy juice." I looked at her and blurted out, "I don't want a painting of me and a monkey!" *What? What? Did I say that out loud?*

The doctor laughed. "Anything else you want to know? Now's the time to ask."

Sister furrowed her brow. "What do you want?"

"The beach. Baby Sister and me at Tybee. The first time we ever saw the ocean."

I'm not sure how long I rambled because I got lost in my beach memory. That summer had been one of my happiest. I was twelve and Baby Sister was seven on what turned out to be our only vacation with Mama and Daddy. After I "came to" at the clinic, Sister never again mentioned a monkey.

What I'd recalled in my stupor was how breaking waves had snatched my beach ball away. I went from chasing my bouncy ball across the sand to standing under the pier with Daddy, already as sunburned as I, waving goodbye to the bright little dot riding bravely toward the horizon. That prized beach ball somehow became my metaphor for death. As loved ones slip out of this life and over the horizon, I see myself standing on the shore waving, while hordes of family and friends who've already gone, gather on the far shore joyously celebrating the new arrivals.

In the pre-*Jaws* era, the vast and mysterious ocean hadn't scared me. I loved to swim. A pool being built in my part of the county was pure fantasy, so I seized every opportunity for jaunts to river shoals, area lakes, and our town pool during the golden weeks it was open. Brother and I usually scrounged the fifteen-cent entry fee from under Mama's couch cushions. Now I wonder if our aunts and uncles accidently-on-purpose lost their loose change there.

Leap forward fifty years and I'd forgotten about swimming. Out of shape and suffering with thoracic nerve damage, my poor body craved exercise. I tried not to envy the flow of runners and bikers passing my house. Unlike me, they were healthy, didn't fear dogs, or seem to need gallons of sunscreen. One day my frustration formed an audible prayer: "God, please give me a sport. Show me something I can do and will enjoy enough to stick with it."

Next thing I knew I was in a pool. A week of morning swims on family vacation reduced my pain more than the prior year of physical therapy. Swimming for fitness had never crossed my mind. Determined to get into the water and move, I came home from vacation and joined the YWCO with its indoor pool. No dogs. No sun. After a month, I swam a few laps. *Go me!* My long-ago physical education teacher had taught me well. After three months, I surprised myself and swam a half mile in a half hour. Not fast, just consistent. That's been my regimen for a year now. Almost every day. Pure joy. Exactly what I'd asked for.

Sister is as proud of my renewed health as I am of the portrait she ultimately painted for me. *Beach Vacation '61* is a gem—Daddy saying "cheese" behind the camera while Mama, Baby Sister, and I pose in the dunes. Holding my lively, briefly-owned beach ball, I feel the heat of sunburn on my shoulders and my heels sinking into the sand. The air tastes salty and the mighty Atlantic thunders behind us.

And you know what else? There's not a monkey in sight.

Chapter 18

The Un-Romance

I'm not romantic," the professor stated with scientific certainty, chin jutted out under his trim gray beard.

"What's romance?" his date asked, disillusioned from her own failed marriage.

"Oh, you know," he said. His face touched her hair as he encircled her with his arms. "Women expect things like candy and flowers. They want poetry, rubies, diamonds, and emeralds."

Glancing around her sparse apartment, she said, "You see where twenty years of that stuff got me, don't you?" She considered the box of cards stashed in the back of her closet. Purchased sentiments, each signed by her ex, *I know I don't show it, but I love you.* Over the course of that lopsided relationship, she'd thrown out more gaudy containers of Valentine candy than Weight Watchers could count. Dozens of roses had hung their heavy heads in sympathy for her. "What makes you say you aren't romantic?" she asked this new man in her life.

"I've been told," he said, spine stiffening.

"Theory or proof?"

A rueful laugh escaped as he relaxed back into the sofa. "I believe there was sufficient data."

She snuggled her head comfortably into the cleft of his shoulder. "I must not be romantic, either. Gifts are often demands in disguise."

He kissed her then, and they stepped in complete accord from dating to loving.

Their un-romance brought her newfound freedom. "Stop trying to guess where I want to eat dinner," he would say, tipping up her chin to look into her eyes. "I asked where *you* wanted to go."

Valentine's Day was a non-event. A week later, he held half-priced chocolates in his teeth and kissed her with each bite. "I'll never bring you flowers," he warned. "What would I say—here, I killed these for you?"

Her green-thumbed friends noticed her blossom along with the kitchen as he turned her canisters into plant stands.

Having reached the age of forty without ever sleeping in a tent, she awoke in the hush of the Rockies to find her man impersonating St. Francis. Small birds perched on his shoulder while he flipped pancakes on a camp stove. The first time she brushed away tentacles of Spanish moss on a pre-dawn trip into the heart of the Okefenokee and clambered onto a platform the size of a postage stamp, she wondered if she had lost her mind. He calmly explained the granddaddy gator they had disturbed had no way of knowing she wasn't part of the platform, and he wasn't about to gobble the whole thing.

Her unromantic man tucked a mug of hot coffee between her mittens and turned her face to the horizon. "Watch," he whispered.

She caught her breath as onyx-black swamp water transformed into ruby whorls hugging bony Cypress knees. Towering trees dripped with what she realized were silver strands of graceful moss.

She hauled wedding attire all the way across the United States and back without ever taking it from the confines of its garment bag. Their vague plan to find a wedding chapel in Las Vegas fell by the wayside after a sweltering week at the Grand Canyon. Marriage license in hand, they opted for the Bureau of Civil Marriages across from the Las Vegas courthouse. Wed in rumpled camping shorts, they were back in the car before their parking meter expired. She has trouble remembering their anniversary without a peek at the license and still laughs over the witness being a rubber stamp.

A trip to a conference in the south of Spain was designated as their honeymoon. After a missed train left them overnight in the scenic village of Alora, they strolled cobblestone streets worn smooth by centuries of footsteps. He broke into a silly old folk song, waxing poetic by adding sillier verses of his own. Overcome with laughter, she collapsed onto the buttress of an ancient stone bridge beneath the diamond-filled night sky.

The next day, they played with Barbary apes, roamed the Kasbah, and chased camels on a North African beach. Stretched out on a ferry crossing back to Gibraltar from Morocco, the new husband suddenly bolted to his feet, energized with a certain spark of discovery. "They say the sun flashes green when it sets over the Atlantic," he shouted. "Let's go see!"

Amused locals made way for them on the starboard railing. Through the Strait of Gibraltar, over the vast ocean toward home, the blazing ball of solar fire disappeared with a flash of pure emerald. That nanosecond of clarity imprinted briefly on her retina and permanently in her unromantic heart.

Chapter 19

Fiasco Muffins

Recently at an internet café, I sat laptop to laptop with fellow writer, Donna, as she munched a nutty, fruity, homemade muffin. "That looks delicious," I commented.

"Healthy, too," she said. "I'll email you the recipe." Simple as a mouse-click *Heart Helper Muffins* came into my life.

They were enticing in simplicity, but I saw right away that oatmeal and apples were the only main ingredients already at home in my cupboard. I am not an adventurous cook. I don't "zest" and will shy away from any recipe involving a calculator. As much as I love my grandmother's Japanese Fruitcake, her instructions that begin "allow three days" never see the light of day in my kitchen. Donna's yummy, easy-sounding muffins were just my speed, so I went happily grocery shopping.

I expected a full-blown search for the healthy items called for amongst the unhealthy stuff I usually buy. As luck would have it, though, this trip also coincided with my go-to grocery store's renovation. All the aisle signs were temporarily down. Walnuts and flour were in their same spots, but without the humongous *BAKING NEEDS* sign swinging over them, I got confused. Resorting to customer service to ferret out cranberries, I suffered a clerk's "that-is-out-of-season" eye roll—an expression well remembered from a Christmas quest to buy a porch swing.

After I finished racing around the store collecting my loot, the cashier discovered a tear in my bag of whole wheat flour. A la Hansel and Gretel, and about as pink-cheeked with embarrassment at holding up the checkout line, I retraced my path of dribbled flour back through the store to get another bag. Since I am a stress eater, I found it hard to resist a rogue impulse to grab a bag of chocolate chips. Victorious, I dashed home—only to find my husband standing in the kitchen munching our very last apple! Unwilling to trudge back to the store, I declared our surviving banana as healthy as the apple.

With the recipe propped up high enough to read without my glasses, I morphed into full-blown chemist mode. I measured, poured, stirred, combined, and folded.

Thinking the mixture was a bit skimpy as I spooned it into greased muffin tins, I figured it would rise. Pleased with my effort, I shoved the pans into the oven, set the timer, and went to clean up the counter.

Removing the recipe from the tall box where I had so handily propped it, I found myself locked into a staring match with the Quaker oats man. I forgot to add the oat-meal!

I fell into a particular state of overdrive that comes with parenthood, that knee-jerk reaction to a child in danger. Out came the pans, dump went the batter, stir went the oatmeal, wash-grease-refill went the pans, and *bang* went the oven door—again.

Ding-ding-ding went the timer.

I had set the timer the first time the muffins went into the oven. Now it served as a signal that my stress had reached an unhelpful heart level. Anyone want to share a bag of chocolate chips?

Heart Helper Muffins

1 egg
3/4 cup fat-free half & half
3 T canola or olive oil
1/3 cup Splenda or sugar
1 med apple, peeled and chopped
3/4 cup dried or fresh cranberries, or raisins
1/2 cup whole wheat flour
1 cup quick-cooking oats
1/4 t salt
1 T baking powder
1/2 t nutmeg
2 t cinnamon

Preheat oven to 450 degrees.
Beat together egg, half & half, & Splenda or sugar.
In a larger bowl, combine remaining ingredients.
Fold egg mixture into dry mixture, just to moisten.
Fill non-stick muffin tins 3/4 full.
Bake 15-20 minutes
ENJOY!

Chapter 20

The Happiness of Art

I pulled away from a stop sign before my brain registered, *"Wings!"* No way.

I drove around the block and what do you know, the signpost had sprouted a beautiful set of crocheted wings. My friend thought they were eyes, another said leaves, but I saw them as multi-colored wings. Textile art, these happy "yarn bombs" had shown up all over town. If I could figure out who the bombers were, I'd ask them to hit my street.

Growing up, my idea of public art rose to the level of stone birdbaths and pottery hens with chicks. Occasionally, a mill wheel or a cemetery angel found its way into someone's yard. I marveled at these creations because my family's public art began and ended with a fancy arbor for Mama's climbing roses. What has stuck with me all these years is not the kind of roses she grew, but her elation at having art in her yard.

Fortune smiled when I came to work in Athens, Georgia. My assigned parking was in the lot beside The Last Resort. I zipped my '66 Corvair into its space and stared. A cutaway mural of vegetables grew up to the roof of the restaurant, their roots sprouting all the way back down to where I stood, gawking. Even on dreary days, under my Beatles-era bubble umbrella, I'd take a moment to enjoy the mural and center myself for the day. My touchstone. Fifty years later, I'm still visiting those giant veggies, circling by to check on the Phoenix while I'm at it. Rising in brilliance from a retaining wall, that bird makes me glad to be alive.

A mundane errand last week turned out to be not so mundane after all when I met a woman driving an art car. Her vehicle was covered bumper to bumper with pithy sayings and glued tchotchkes. I told her how happy it made me. To which, she quipped, "It's really to make *me* happy."

Since happiness is the benchmark, my uncle was well on his way to having an art car when he took a four-inch paintbrush to his Ford Galaxy and gave it a coat of robin's egg blue.

Suddenly, I imagined my Prius encrusted with wide bands of sparkling gems, one color blending into the next. I'd be driving a rainbow! My practical side piped up about cars not lasting forever. Okay, but if you see a rainbow drive by, it's probably me.

Last year, a pair of defunct payphone stands near my home went from ignored, to yarn bombed, to whimsical cupcakes. In February, they cuddled as symbols of love. I looked forward to what came next and wasn't disappointed. They stood naked as the day their phones were removed—vintage art that I hadn't appreciated. Naked was their cocoon phase, because now they've morphed into a butterfly. Pulling in for a closer look, I caught my reflection in the rear-view mirror. I saw the same goofy grin my ninety-year-old cousin wore when a butterfly settled on his lapel.

Around here scrap metal is raw material for sculpture. Creatures known and unknown, fanciful dogs, snakes, and dragons dot our landscape. Lifelike, swinging and swaying on rusty springs and hinges, they get my heart racing. Utility repurposed as art. Like Mama's rose arbor, and the railroad trestle downtown, after it graced the cover of REM's *Murmur* album.

Athens greets the public with statues of decorated bulldogs, an elegant Athena, plus artisan bus shelters. But we lost the Iron Horse. From the moment UGA's Art Department unveiled him, the two-ton beast endured the indignities of vandalism and snickered through attempts to burn him down. Now though, this "Pegasus without

Wings" is displayed in a neighboring county with his hiney toward our fine city. Can't say as I blame him.

At the Botanical Gardens, an 815-pound sphere of solid black marble is etched with Earth's continents and floats on a micro-thin sheet of water. Children and adults go from disbelief to glee as they discover they can spin the world.

Why not? Stop signs are growing wings.

Chapter 21

Story Shopping

I save time when I pay for gas at the pump, bank online, and order books with a mouse click but all this technology cheats me out of stories. Every fall I go shopping for them—dorm, garage, yard, tag, estate, neighborhood, moving, down-sizing—any folksy sale will do. When families sort out basements and attics, memories they have packed away also emerge. The stories I find are priceless even if the treasures aren't.

People love reminiscing about when and why they acquired an item, recapturing one last time the pleasure it brought. I took a weathered decoy off the hands of a blind gentleman who used to hunt in the northern lake country. I will never huddle in a duck blind waiting for a hapless flock of mallards to fly over, but he gave me a good understanding of what it's like as he ran his fingers over his cherished object.

I am flooded with images of places I haven't been when I see collectibles from across the globe: Korean lantern, Russian trickster toy, Eskimo drum, Indian sandalwood carving, hand-woven African basket, certified piece of Ireland's Blarney Stone, Spanish peacock fan. Each has its story. I learned about Austria by merely reaching out to steady an art-glass vase. There is no limit to what can be sold at garage sales, including the garage itself. Rule of thumb, though: you must first own it. One man turned as red as the wagon he was selling when a neighbor informed him it belonged to her children.

Needlework pieces have memories stitched into them and vintage aprons prompt cooks to divulge guarded family recipes. Not only do I hang onto the stories, but the names of previous owners. Nellie Wood is my handy grab-it that reaches for things. Maude-Olive, a vintage rocking chair from an estate sale, resides in my granddaughter's nursery like a dependable nanny.

A yard sign that read *Take Them--They're Hers* forewarned me of a somebody-done-somebody-wrong story. Another day, a wife sold me a bicycle for almost nothing after her husband priced it sky high and then ran off to play golf instead of helping her with the sale. Conversely, a husband unhappily left in charge gave everything away rather than miss an impending kickoff. I was amused by a man carping about parts he forgot to include with some gadget he had sold. The third time he complained, "I'm telling you it won't *work* without these," his wife suggested a couple of things he could do with them.

At a post-moving sale, a couple offered tours of their new home. I commented on its peaceful atmosphere, and they said, "That's because of the Spirit. When it was being framed our church wrote scripture all over it."

I took that idea to my sister who was in the throes of renovating an old Victorian manse we had dubbed "Honey's Spook House." We covered its aged bones with Bible verses and dispelled any ghosts lurking there.

I meet memorable people, like a young man convincing a woman *not* to sell her sterling flatware to him, a coed who burst out laughing when she found herself haggling over a quarter, and a youth whose shaved scalp had tattoos of jigsaw puzzle pieces.

Arriving at an especially well-attended estate sale one October morning, I wedged my car between two pine trees and trekked up the driveway. I reached the house as an elderly man bolted out the front door and reeled down the steps. "Saw all these cars," he gasped. "Thought Old Doc had died!"

The juxtaposition of random articles sparks my imagination. At one sale, I was so distracted by a toy lizard wearing a silver earring I stumbled over a paper bag and set off blood-chilling rattling sounds. Rattlesnake skins!

I immediately turned to get the story from the dignified matron holding the sale. Hands folded atop her ebony cane, she rolled her eyes to heaven and said, "Don't *even* ask."

Oh, how I wish I had.

Chapter 22

Caught with My Britches Down

Back when Bill Gates and Steve Jobs were still teenagers, I connected to the universe via the wall phone in my kitchen. My busy life tied that phone's long spiral tether into knots. One fateful morning, I received a call and then placed another in quick succession.

"Helen," I said when my neighbor answered, "you won't believe what our *new best friend* wanted this morning." With the receiver sandwiched between my shoulder and chin, I swiped oatmeal off my toddler's face and transferred him from the highchair to the playpen. "She asked me to take her to Kmart for a spool of thread."

"Good grief!" Helen was indignant. "And you with a sick baby."

She and I had met brooding Betty that summer when our families moved into her subdivision. Three young mothers with first-graders, we carpooled, but the school year was barely underway before Helen and I realized we were Betty's only friends.

"Heads up, she'll call you next."

"She could borrow thread from her mother-in-law. She just wants to get away from home."

"True," I said. "Her husband is out of work again. She doesn't seem to have a kind word for either of her poor children—"

"*Genie?*" Betty's raspy voice sliced into our conversation like a buzz saw. Inexplicably, her line had remained connected to mine from our previous call. "Are you and Helen talking about me?"

Helen gasped. I dropped my receiver. As I stared at the phone cord uncoiling itself, I felt the full force of a funny warning I'd heard all my life: "Don't get caught with your britches down." Well, I was caught, so exposed my britches might as well have been around my ankles. And it wasn't funny. Betty never spoke to me again. Imagine the shame I felt the next year when she was charged with child abuse. Yes, she was needy—she had needed me.

I should have learned enough from Betty to have recognized Sue. I can only blame intervening years, my family's relocation, and the new career I launched after my children were in college. Sue elected herself my *new best friend* and insisted on taking me to lunch. She picked me up in her minivan, so I had no escape when her marital woes started pouring out.

After that lunch, I dodged her calls. Forever in crisis, she drained what little energy I had left from my hectic days. "Gee, Sue, we're just sitting down to dinner," I lied one evening. My already-fed husband raised a quizzical brow. "You don't know her," I grumbled. "She's too needy."

Sue stopped calling, and I forgot about her. But God didn't forget about her—or me.

One crisp fall day, I rushed home from an errand that took twice as long as expected and drove a route I rarely use. Slowing at a bridge over the Oconee River, I was astounded to see Sue sitting atop the narrow railing, leaning toward the rapids below.

Was I ever caught with my britches down! Again. Prideful self-involvement had caused me to withhold friendship from this woman. Dialing 911, I pulled onto the riverbank beside her minivan and bolted back across the bridge shouting, "Sue! Sue! Wait!"

Passing traffic whipped her long auburn hair. Her pretty face was etched with pain. "Go away," she yelled.

I shook my head. "I can't."

We were both in a terrible place; unsure how we got there, much less how to get out.

A burly young policeman with wisdom beyond his years arrived. He blocked traffic with his cruiser and eased up on foot behind Sue. Like the troll from *Three Billy Goats Gruff*, he roared, "*What are you doing on my bridge?*" and yanked her backward, off the railing. Thumping the pack of cigarettes in her shirt pocket, he said, "Ma'am, if you jump you'll get your smokes wet, and that'll really make you mad."

Sue blinked, and then she started laughing. We laughed until we cried and then cried until, friends at last, we were laughing again.

Eventually, Sue moved on to a happier place in another state. And I moved on to practice what I had learned—I never meet a needy person that I don't mentally hitch up my britches and wonder if they need me.

Section III

I speak in stories, they represent Life itself.
Genie Smith Bernstein

Chapter 23

Doing the Wash

Water sprayed the clothes as I dropped them into the washer and my tears flowed in with them. There was barely a load, my son had packed the rest. Engorged duffels. Army green, official, and bound for the other side of the globe.

I was proud but my heart, my broken heart, knew the truth. My boy was gone. He would come home a man. This was a good thing, right? All those times he and I read *The Jack Tales* about how Jack went off to slay giants and seek his fortune, I never once considered Jack's mother.

Before dropping the last shirt into the washer, I used it to stem fresh tears. He was there. A trace of cologne his sister gave him reminded me of yesterday's good-bye. Bending from his lofty height to embrace me on tiptoe, each holding onto the other fiercely, treasuring it up in our hearts. "Mom," he'd said, eyes brimming, "I love you. You've always been there for me."

"And I always will be," I declared, knowing I would die trying. Knowing he was going far beyond my reach.

How did my mother bear it when my brother left for Viet Nam? How long did she cry into the tub of her old Kenmore on the back porch? When Daddy went overseas with Patton, did my grandmother's tears run through the wringer of her machine? In turn, had her own mother's heart spilled onto her washboard over the son called into World War I? And the Civil War. How many matriarchs in my family stood in yards and bawled into cast iron wash pots as their boys marched away?

I sank down on the little bench beside my washer and tried to figure out how this had slipped up on me. He had spent eight months in training and had earned a uniform full of decorations. When I admired his "Expert" medal for grenades, he'd laughed. "That one was easy. Once you pull the pin out of a grenade, it's *no problem at all* to throw it three miles."

I looked down at his tee shirt in my hands. *I don't have to wash it today.*

His soccer ball had been my undoing. When I moved the car into the garage, and he didn't bring out his bags, I'd gone back into the house and found him kneeling on the ball, forcing air out of it. With a familiar hand-in-the-cookie-jar grin, he had mumbled something about having room and maybe needing it. My mind's eye saw him as an eight-year-old on our way to the first of what turned out to be a decade of soccer fields. I remember saying, "I don't know a thing about soccer, do you?"

"Nope." His grin that day wrinkled his freckled nose as he held tightly to that first soccer ball. Now it was going with him where I could not.

Before getting into the car, he took a farewell romp with the dog. One hundred pounds of shepherd frolicking with one hundred and seventy-five pounds of boy--soldier--man. As we drove across Athens, I tried not to see him drinking in all his familiar places, memories to cherish when he was far away. The ram's horn that synagogues sound on Rosh Shoshanna is symbolic of Sarah crying out in agony when Abraham took Isaac to the mountain. I understood. I could have made that sound.

So here I sit, face buried in a faded tee shirt, praying desperately for God to help me, as he had helped my predecessors. The phone in the kitchen rang, piercing my misery. I ran to answer and heard my daughter ask cheerfully, "Would you like to borrow my boy for the weekend?"

What better tonic than a six-year-old? I stepped back to the laundry room, tossed the wadded shirt into the washer, and slammed the lid. "You bet! I'm on my way."

Chapter 24

Going Batty

Okay, bats are useful, and my garage is admittedly cave-like, but three years is my limit for sweeping guano. Luckily, I live near the Georgia Museum of Natural History, a rare gem at the University of Georgia. One phone call brought me a bat expert. She gauged my unwanted guests as a handful of big brown bats in the habit of resting beside my back door, digesting their nightly forages. A visiting few was light years better than the vast colony of little black critters I had imagined taking up residence. But it didn't solve the guano problem.

As I launched into research on how to make my garage less Halloween-ish all year long, a fellow writer's voice rang in the back of my mind: '*You know, life is re-search.*' That'd been his answer to my frustration one summer when travel left me without time to write. His remark coincided with my husband's animal-behavior conference, so I conducted a seat-of-the-pants field study. From unkempt locks to Birkenstocks, those scientists opened my eyes and enriched my writing.

Insatiable curiosity was apparent from the get-go when the keynote speaker from Los Angeles failed to show up. Half a continent away, he kept his colleagues enthralled with the birth watch for his baby, the first giant panda born in the United States. Since the miracle of new life transcends language and culture, it was the perfect opening for an international conference. Yes, I know, bat pups are adorable, too. I just don't want any.

All I need to spark passion in a character is to re-member the intensity in the dark eyes of a young woman who studied monkeys. Specifically, the role of scrotal color in mate selection. As incredible as that sounds, there's probably someone observing the same thing about bats. The data she presented at her seminar kept the audi-ence spellbound, and I swear every man there checked his fly.

One willowy scientist with a platinum mane looked like a fashion model, but modeled shyness instead. More at ease in the Congo than in the classroom, she found people uncomfortable, but not the bug she had hosted in her ear for nine weeks. Sad about drowning the poor thing by trying to wash it out, she planned to hold a flashlight to her ear next time, so it could crawl back up the canal. Next time? Crawl up the what? Could I reverse her idea and use light to uninvite my bats?

The survival instinct is obvious in bats, as it was in one seasoned professor I met at the conference. The previous night, he'd ducked under a table while a shotgun-wielding robber held up the restaurant where he was dining. To everyone's amazement, our friend had resumed his meal afterward. "I've been living on boiled cabbage and rice in Tanzania," he explained. "I'm not leaving a steak on the table."

When my characters face adversity, I recall a handsome graduate student. He followed the same rigorous schedule as everyone else, rushing in, slinging his backpack off his shoulder, and scrambling to take notes. A bat in his situation would perish, but this young man, born without arms, accomplished more with his teeth and toes than most humans with all four appendages.

One self-described, nutty professor tested cortisol levels in scat. He was an exemplar of surprising good humor and mischief. Legendary for getting exotic samples through customs, he rocked back on his heels and grinned like a "mule eatin' briars" about agents who never quite believed his bags were full of—y'know—guano.

My little study proved *Life is Research*. Now I take a breath and take notes whenever time constraints threaten a creative drought. And I've learned a hefty spritz of ammonia at dusk discourages bats from hanging out in my garage. Now that I understand my little skeeter-eaters better, though, I don't spray every night. Sweeping isn't such a chore.

Happy Halloween!

Chapter 25

Catnapping

Genie? Genie Smith!" A classmate from thirty years ago hailed my high school name through his open car window. "You asleep?"

My eyes flew open and I snatched up the *Vote for Kate* campaign sign leaning against my leg. "No!" I lied. "Just catnapping."

I had been fast asleep, chin in hand with elbow propped on the arm of a chair.

He drove away laughing. That had been one of his signature moves in high school.

I glanced over at the big tabby on the ivy-covered steps behind me. Her family had barely driven out of sight that primary morning when she deigned to join my campaign vigil on the library corner across from her house. Big Cat stretched and smirked at my embarrassment.

Once I recovered from being caught sleeping on the job, I waved my sign with gusto. I hoped the old friend who'd shouted my schoolgirl name had cast his vote for our classmate running for county reelection.

On her way to my side of the street, Big Cat had stopped in the middle to roll and perform her morning ablutions. She'd twitched her tail with irritation at early voters maneuvering their vehicles too close. One of those was the local banker, Bob, and his wife, Mary. They gave me a thumbs-up. Mary soon walked back, grumbling that she'd forgotten her ID, and Bob was making her walk back home to get it.

Allied with me all day, Big Cat threaded between my feet as I stood smiling *like a mule eatin' briars* and waving my sign. When I sat down in my lawn chair, she passed beneath, bumping me with her arched back.

I'd voted absentee in my county in order to be on this hometown corner promoting my friend. "I hope you'll vote for Kate," I shouted, turning her red-white-and-blue name toward a battered pickup rounding the corner.

"Oh, we will," the young man said with a grin. "We don't know much about her politics—"

"Yeah—" His wife finished his sentence with a giggle, "—she married us." Their truck putt-putted away with what appeared to be a single occupant.

Politics. I understand the democratic necessity of re-placing those in office who work against the public good. But Kate, a proven public servant who makes a real difference in this community, would lose her job without enough people affirming her with their votes today.

Back when she first stepped into the political arena, my husband drove her in the county parade. We had borrowed a 1969 Mercedes convertible, a beauty with its original aquamarine finish. Scrambling to take our place in the parade line, Kate and I slapped her magnetic campaign signs onto the car. PLOP! They hit the dirt, and we fell into helpless laughter. Duh? 1969—Fiberglass body!

Big Cat interrupted a set of calisthenics to amble over and see what I was chuckling about. A muddy truck, hauling its work crew to lunch, slowed at the corner to let two men jump off the back. I held up my sign and said, "I hope you're going to vote."

They smiled, and one man missing a front tooth, lisped, "We thure are." He gestured toward my sign. "We had her in thixth grade." Watching them lope up the hill, I considered Kate's decade of teaching and his positive slant on *what goes around, comes around.*

A surge of voters arrived after work. I bobbed my sign enthusiastically, and they either nodded or averted their eyes. What if Kate didn't get enough votes? As the polls closed, I folded my campaign tent. Big Cat bolted home.

Trudging to the courthouse at dusk, I removed the posters I'd put up at daybreak. As precincts reported in, I was struck by the numbers. I'm used to votes in the thousands. Some of these never reached a hundred. Thankfully, Kate prevailed. She carried the precinct where I spent the day by ten votes. *Ten.* If Mary hadn't walked home for her ID, or the married couple had opted for romance, or the former students had eaten lunch with their buddies, that margin would have narrowed to *five.*

I've toyed with the idea that, in the grand political scheme, my measly vote doesn't count. Witnessing that grass-roots process, I regained appreciation of how precious my ballot is. I'm not going to be caught catnapping again.

Chapter 26

My Mother's Day Gift

My corsage sat askew but I didn't care. My son was away from home, and he had sent it to me for Mother's Day. In a hurry to reach church on time, I drove my usual route, barely noticing the snowy dogwoods in yards or the azaleas flaming around the foundations of homes.

A young man, however, did catch my eye. He was in a hurry too. About the same age as my son, he bore the rumpled look of a boy learning to manage on his own. He scurried from a student apartment with his Sunday coat dangling precariously from a hanger, best shoes clutched in his other hand, key ring gripped between his teeth.

I smiled and wondered if he was off to see his mom

or if she had "raised him right" and he was headed to church. The mother in me telepathically admonished, "Not a good idea," when he flung his shoes on top of his car to fumble with the lock. My experience of losing the new tag for my car in that exact manner, with just a quick trip to the store for screws to put the thing on, was fresh in my mind.

He failed to pick up my transmitted warning. I stopped at a red light down the block and looked for his car in the rearview mirror. It zipped out his driveway with two brown lumps clearly defined on the roof.

I pulled away from the light and watched him barrel up behind me. He was poised to swing into the left lane for a quick pass then disappear, leaving me to deal with the demise of his leather loafers. One had already rolled over and the other sat facing the wind. Their moments were numbered.

I punched on my emergency flasher and bumped onto the shoulder of the road. If this young man was indeed raised right, he was not going to pass by me and my corsage on Mother's Day without lending a hand. Sure enough, he pulled alongside. Stretching a lanky arm across his passenger seat, he cranked the window open and called out, "You have a problem?"

I shook my head, jabbed my finger overhead a few times, and shouted back, "You do."

He lifted a quizzical brow.

"Shoes!"

He thunked himself soundly on his noggin, put the car in neutral, and grappled out his window until he snagged his footwear. Throwing the car back in gear, he gave me a sturdy thumbs-up and scooted off down the road, probably to the brink of his next self-made disaster. Because someone, I choose to think it was his mother, raised him right, he got a little help this time.

Watching a wave of cruciform blossoms from a nearby dogwood drift across my windshield, I readjusted the shoulder belt around my corsage. "Oh, God," I sighed, "let me have raised my son right. Thank you for peopling this world with others who may reach out to him when I can't."

Chapter 27

Daddy Sits on The Right

Unless we four children were running fevers or dead on Sunday mornings, we sat beside Daddy on the third pew from the back on the right-hand side of the First Baptist Church in our little town. Like clockwork, he'd back the *Old Black Roach* out of the garage and look over his Sunday School lesson while Mama got our sashes tied, cowlicks spit down, and her earrings screwed on. It was a tussle, but we usually ended up on time, Bibles in hand, tie or crinoline straight, socks cuffed right side out, clutching dimes for the collection plate.

The day Daddy tried to take us all by himself was a disaster. Mama was sick, so we got each other ready as best we could and piled into the car. Halfway to town, Baby Sister bounced into Sister's lap.

"Daddy, stop!" Sister screamed. "We have to go back home."

"What's wrong?" he said, stomping the brake.

"Baby Sister doesn't have on panties."

Glancing at his toddler, prettily put together in her pale green organza dress and shiny black Mary Jane's, Daddy said, "Oh, that's all right. Nobody will know."

"*No!*" I couldn't believe Sister risked her life by aiming a "*no*" directly at Daddy. "Kids in that nursery stand on their *heads*," she cried.

I held my breath while Daddy pulled off the road. He gave Sister a long look that included the little tomboy wriggling in her lap, green satin bow already sliding out of her topknot. He sighed and turned the car around.

When we got home, Mama told us Auntie, to whom we'd waved on her way to church, hadn't been waving. She was trying to flag us down with Baby's panties.

One year, on the way to Thanksgiving service, somebody fired a BB gun just as we crossed the Little River Bridge. The BB lodged in the window glass a hair short of Brother's eyeball. None of us had to be at church that day to be thankful.

Every Mother's Day, though, we were all about blind by the time we got there. Daddy stood us out in the bright Georgia sun in front of Grandma's crape myrtle and handed one of us the end of a knotted string. When he got the distance measured to the right knot, we'd drop the string and stare into the sunlight however long it took for him to get a good picture. On those Sundays, he'd cut red rose buds for our lapels in honor of Mama, and he'd wear a white one in memory of Grandma. Mama fussed the year he pinned pink buds on us, saying that meant she was half dead.

The Sunday she only put on one earring, she was hopping mad when not one of us—Daddy included—hadn't noticed on the way to church. Brother's fate was pointing it out on the way back home.

When I was twelve, Daddy made two giant wooden tablets with the Ten Commandments carved on them for Auntie. She ran the Junior Department at church—and anything else they'd let her, Mama said—and she couldn't have made a bigger to-do over those tablets if they'd been stone straight from Moses.

Everything that came out of Daddy's workshop was special. We weren't allowed inside, but we'd skip along while he carried boards up and down the hill. Whenever he drew on pieces of wood with his big flat pencil, somebody was in for a surprise. Mama got pine-paneling in the dining room one Christmas, and I got a whole house the summer Baby was born. My playhouse had a front porch, windows you could really raise, and rooms full of doll furniture. Not a week went by that somebody on their way to Atlanta didn't stop and try to buy my house for their little girl.

Auntie displayed her Ten Commandments in the Junior Department on a table draped with purple velvet. During devotionals, I'd peek at those rules Daddy carved. I knew he lived by them. And he expected me to as well.

After Sunday school, we'd find Mama and Daddy in the sanctuary on that third pew from the back on the right-hand side. When I was in eighth grade, friends asked me to sit in the balcony. Daddy said okay, but before I hit the stairs, I found the girls giggling beside the front door. We ran to the corner drugstore, spent the worship hour drinking vanilla Cokes, and slipped back into church on the last amen. I was thrilled with my daring adventure until Daddy turned the nose of our new Chevrolet toward home. Spying the top of the towering White Oak in our yard, I realized there was no way we'd get there without Daddy asking me about the church service. I was going to have to lie. *LIE!* I did what I always did when I didn't know what else to do. I cried.

After we children were grown and gone, we lost Mama, but Daddy never failed to be in his appointed place on Sunday morning. Often my brother and sisters and enough of our children showed up to overflow that third pew from the back on the right-hand side.

Arriving late from Athens, I scurried past the greeters and snatched open the door to that right-hand aisle. An alert usher caught me, literally, by the scruff of my neck. "Your Daddy isn't over here," he whispered.

"Where is he?" I asked, accusatorily, like he'd misplaced him.

He nodded diagonally across the sanctuary. "Easier to hear up there."

Astounded, I spotted Daddy on the *fifth* pew from the *front* on the *left*. I eased across the back of the auditorium, more than a little disoriented. Even on my long-ago wedding day, when he'd set off down the aisle with me, I'd half expected us to turn in at that third pew from the back on the right-hand side.

I walked self-consciously up the left aisle and slipped in beside him. The feeling of being out of place disappeared as soon as a tickle in my throat produced a peppermint from his pocket, same as always.

Daddy's health declined until he rarely had an opportunity to be in church. The last Father's Day I found him there, we sang hymns and shared an inspired sermon based on Jesus' saying, "Let the children come to me."

Chapter 28

Uh Oh Turkey O

My grandson ran ahead of me at the grocery store, hunting the candies we'd need to assemble our whimsical turkey treats—a candy corn beak, pushed into a microwave softened square of caramel body, perched on pecan half feet, with a fudge-stripe cookie tail. The trick is to assemble all at once, before the caramel re-hardens. Simple and silly, but a whole flock on a tray is striking, or a few on other dishes adds a decorative touch. Plus, they're yummy! But I hadn't realized they were tradition until I saw an adult granddaughter's lip poke out last Thanksgiving when I didn't make them.

I grabbed two bags of fudge-stripe cookies, a pound

of pecan halves, and caught up with my spirited four-year-old at a freezer bin piled with the real things. While I chose a turkey to roast, my companion decided to share his newest joke, punchline and all. "Y'know what's a turkey's favorite day of the year? The day *after* Thanksgiving!"

We laughed, and I flashed back to when I was his age, frightened by the ear-splitting brakes that halted the freight train passing my childhood home. Brother, the guilty party who put the penny on the tracks, fled. Sister hauled me out of the way as the engineer disembarked and Mama met him midway in the yard. I quaked, imagining what punishment would rain down on children who stopped trains. Mama and the engineer exchanged smiles and then money for one of the turkeys that we were fattening up in a pen near the tracks. My mouth was still hanging open when the train rumbled around the bend with a happy whistle and its Thanksgiving prize.

I watched my pint-sized assistant try to wrestle the fat bird I bagged into the shopping cart and chuckled over my friend Anne's stinking Thanksgiving. She procured her turkey and trimmings in a mad dash squeezed into one of last week's lunch hours. Stopping quickly at her house, Anne flung the grocery bag containing the turkey in the freezer and dropped the one filled with cans of chicken broth onto the floor. Or so she thought. Turns out, the broth was frozen solid, and her house was soon filled with the stench of thawed and rotting turkey.

Not at all what came to my mind the spring I unwittingly drove between two wild toms "duking it out" over a flock of hens in my neighborhood. The males beautifully fanned their tail-feathers and strutted into the street. Forced to stop, I stuck my phone out the window to take pictures. One launched an attack on my front bumper, flogging it with outstretched wings and jolting the tires with powerful pecks. The other went for my phone, telescoping his neck, viciously snapping his beak at me as the window slid upward—seemingly in slow motion. Those toms became such a nuisance they ended up as dinner at the homeless shelter. I hope they were as tasty as they were pretty.

My determined youngster won his turkey-wrestling match just as a woman bustled up to the bin. "You're mighty strong," she complimented him. Selecting hers, she added, "It's not Thanksgiving without a turkey."

Oddly, because of my friend, Kim's, experience, that remark reminded me to pick up macaroni. Kim's three small children had been looking forward to mac & cheese for their holiday meal one year when family finances were tight. A shopper who eyed their sparse cart, thoughtlessly commented, "You forgot the turkey. You have to have a turkey for Thanksgiving."

On their drive home from the store, Kim's older son decided God would give him a turkey if he prayed for one. Not to be left out, his little brother also prayed for one. On a roll, they prayed for a third turkey for their ba-

by sister, plus one for Mom, and one for Dad. Astonish-
ing as it sounds, five turkeys, from five unrelated sources,
arrived at their door by Thanksgiving. The children were
not the least bit surprised.

Loading groceries into the car, my helper spied his
backpack. "I made you turkeys," he announced, pulling
out a tracing of his handprints brightly painted as gob-
blers. Clasping the little hands that made those prints, I
hoped someday they'd be making candy turkey treats for
his grandchildren.

Chapter 29

In Search of Perfection

Nothing is perfect, they say. Well, it's the gospel truth when it comes to purses, lipsticks, and hair styles. I know. My wallet is as empty as all the promises I've fallen for.

It took physical therapy to unkink my back from the weight of so many bad shoulder bags. Like the inimitable Erma Bombeck, if someone in the family thought they might need an anvil, I'd have had to carry it in my purse. Alone in a deserted parking lot one night, I scrabbled in the depths of my handbag for the car keys. The door stubbornly remained locked until closer examination revealed I was trying to open it with my son's Batmobile. My shrieks of laughter surely deterred any lurking danger. My last purse was nearly perfect but I was too short-sighted to buy a gross of it. Not only has it been discontinued but even eBay can't find one for me.

I never saw lipstick as a problem until Avon stopped making its little sample tubes. When I was a teenager, I didn't need to buy lipsticks because there was always a plethora of samples around. Come to think of it, that's probably the reason Avon stopped making its little sample tubes. Our Avon Lady didn't ring the bell and certainly was not a lady. Our representative was a wizened little old dairyman who rapped on door posts county-wide and was such a personable character that women bought his wares in bulk. He could have easily married but was said to be looking for a perfect woman. I finally made a commitment to a color named Sunset. It was perfect. I wore it year-round and it's the only tube I've ever used up completely. I dug out every smidge once I found out it was, of course, discontinued. Too bad lipstick can't be mixed and sold like paint. Too bad a good man has to go through life alone.

I have put color in my lips by biting them like my great aunts did but I never used their trick of rolling in a flower bed for perfume. Their scent was stronger than intended once their impish baby sister decided to feed the chickens there.

My aunts styled each other's hair with a barbaric curling iron contraption. Sneaking his sisters' appliance, my uncle achieved a look more like a corn field postharvest than the Douglas Fairbanks wave he was after.

I learned the pain of imperfect hair styles at an early age. Mama would sit me on the kitchen steps to trim my bangs and then she would morph into a scissors-wielding fiend unable to get them even. When I was thirteen, old enough to object to inch-long bangs, she put a body wave in the top of my hair. Instead of body, I ended up with a crown full of tight curls atop my long golden side tresses. No cocker spaniel ever looked better and I have the school yearbook pictures to prove it.

I don't consider myself vain, but I do have my moments. One that is carved into my forebrain came a few years ago at a party. As I was discussing the finer points of murder and mayhem with a fellow mystery writer, I overheard someone behind me pose a question to my husband. "How do you like Genie's new hairdo?"

You might say I became all ears but, truth be told, I'd been that way all week. I had, in my daddy's vernacular, gotten my ears lowered. I went on a simple errand to the bank on what had to be the hottest day in history when I was struck with an accursed hot flash. Rather than strip and run through the bank's landscape sprinklers, I'd dashed into a beauty shop and exchanged my ponytail for a pixie cut.

I couldn't believe my unfettered ears when I heard my husband answer, "I hate it."

He never uses the "H" word. I've only heard the "L" word slip from his lips twice. A scientist, he is disinclined to ascribe words to feelings, but my naked nape had provided sufficient data. In that moment, I wished I had opted for the sprinklers. Authorities would have likely tucked me away in the catacomb of some institution instead of leaving me free for scrutiny.

There must be scads of things about me that my husband would change if he could, things I can't change. Maturity and first marriages taught us to accept each other as we are. One thing I can do, however, is grow long hair. Wonder how it would look with a body wave, just a small one, right on top...

Chapter 30

Identity Gift

Ever on guard against identity theft, I was amazed to find myself in possession of a brand new identity. It came full-blown the day my granddaughter's teacher hailed across a parking lot, "GG…GiGi…*Gee Gee*." She had to call several times before I realized she meant me. That's not my name, at least I hadn't thought so. I'd been referring to myself as Grandma Genie, abbreviated to GG on postcards and travel blogs, but I hadn't expected it to extend past my family.

Genie—wife, mother, office manager—led a structured existence, whereas the empty-nester and retired GG was extraordinarily free. Some would say unshackled.

Looking back, I believe my grandmothers felt that same liberation from the societal pressures of their day. One took up smoking and the other opened a business. I started writing. A dream come true!

I don't claim to be the sage of old wives' tales, but I do seem to have attained a mite of her status. Along with my wit and wisdom, grandchildren accepted this new persona whole cloth. When a former coworker looked down his nose at my comfy purple Crocs and sniffed, "So, is that the kind of shoes *writers* wear?" my ten-year-old Sir Galahad grandson quipped, "Nope, it's the kind GG wears."

Sharing things I loved as a child allows me to enjoy them again. Put a jump rope and a hula hoop in your garage and you'll see. A kite on a windy day trumps an iPad, and a bicycle still sends imaginations spinning. Teenagers will tell me more over a jigsaw puzzle than I can worm out of them in a week. When presented with a bouquet of little granddaughters, I resurrected a canopy bed and rummaged yard sales for dress-up clothes. In five minutes flat from my front door to the Princess Room, the girls transported to another realm. And they often carried me with them, back to when my sisters and I played 'tend like. The bonus with toddlers is delicious, guilt-free afternoon naps.

Now that conversation has given way to texts and tweets, astute grandmothers pass baskets collecting iPhones instead of baskets of dinner rolls. Technology keeps me in touch with older grandchildren out roaming the globe, while the younger ones try keeping up with all the grandmothers in our extended family. Recently four-year-old Grant recited his: "Nonny, Grandma Shelah, Nana Susan, GG…" he hesitated then added, "…and the pretty lady downstairs."

Startled, his parents said, "Who?"

Grant led them to his playroom and pointed at the big poster of the smiling beauty who watched over him and his train sets. I'm certain the iconic Marilyn Monroe, who would have been in her nineties by now, would embrace the new identity he bestowed upon her as the gift it truly is.

Chapter 31

Favorite Family Recipes

My mouth waters just thinking about my grandmother's Japanese Fruitcake. It weighed about ten pounds and was her special Christmas gift to her children's families. Thankfully, Mama was her daughter and we got one every year.

My long-awaited slice had hand-grated fresh coconut atop perfect Seven-Minute Frosting. Beneath lay one layer of delicious white cake tinted pink, a middle layer with fresh pecans delicately and deliciously spiced, and a yellow melt-in-your-mouth layer on the bottom.

Why it was called Japanese escaped my knowledge, but I looked forward to it every year.

Nanny made and froze her beauties ahead of time. Mama thawed ours in the "sun room," an enclosed porch on the back of our house known as the "pneumonia hole" in winter.

Nanny's recipe, written in her own hand, resides in my recipe box. Every year I get it out, open its aged folds, and read the first line: "Allow Three Days." I take a few minutes to savor precious memories of Nanny and her high standard of cooking. Then, I'm embarrassed to say, I refold her instructions and tuck them back into the box.

I don't approach Nanny Callaway's quality of cooking, but I pass on what I can. Here are a couple of my favorites:

#1 Piggy in a Blanket a la Alex

Four-year-old's spin on old favorite.

Ingredients and Tools:
Can of Crescent Rolls
Kitchen Scissors
Package of Hot Dogs
Granpapa

Directions:
1. Tear paper off a can of crescent rolls and bang on sink until it pops open. (Sort of loud, but fun.)
2. Pull the eight rolls apart. They are triangles. Use scissors to cut each one in half. (Count and be sure you made sixteen blankets.)
3. Get Granpapa to cut eight hot dogs in half. (He calls this dividing. Check to be sure he ends up with sixteen.)
4. Roll each piggy in a blanket and put it on a pan.

(Sing with Granpapa:

> *Roll, roll, roll a piggy,*
> *Gently in the dough.*
> *Merrily, merrily, merrily, merrily*
> *Cook it nice and slow.*)

5. Granpapa will bake them in a 375-degree oven for ten

to twelve minutes. (Long enough to sing "Blue Skies" and practice dancing with him.)

6. After the pan gets cool, put a little hat of catsup on a piggy and eat it. (Yummy!)

7. Decorate the rest and give Granpapa big hugs for helping. (He won't care if you get catsup on him, too.)

#2 Twenty-First-Century Syrup Biscuits

Five-year-old's' variation of his great-grandfather's favorite. (whose call for syrup and biscuits meant supper was a disaster)

Ingredients and Tools:
Canned biscuits
Cinnamon and Sugar
Syrup
Grandma Genie aka GG

Directions:
1. Pull paper of canned biscuits until they pop open. (This is lots of fun.)
2. Put biscuits on a dry pan and make them all touch. (Practice counting.)
3. Sprinkle with cinnamon and sugar. (Lick up what gets on counter.)
4. Ask GG to bake biscuits in 400-degree oven for 8 to 10 minutes. (Any grown-up can help but grandmas bake cookies.)
5. When it won't burn your finger, poke a hole in a biscuit. (Use a finger that has not just petted the dog.)
6. Fill up the hole with syrup and watch it soak in.
(Long enough to sing "Do Re Mi" but not "Knick Knack Paddy Wack.")

7. Fill up the hole with syrup one more time and eat it. (Yummy!)

8. Fix a syrup biscuit for GG and give it to her with a kiss. (She doesn't care if you are sticky.)

Chapter 32

Eli's Angel

FaceBook often shocks me, but nothing like today with the picture of a crushed car and my grandson, Eli, on a stretcher. Before I read he'd escaped serious injury, I knew it. His guardian angel put in a personal appearance when Eli was six.

Back then, I'd clear my schedule when the leap-before-you-look boy was with me. But one morning, I *needed* to attend Weight Watchers and celebrate my hard-fought pounds lost. I searched for light-weight clothes while Eli licked cream cheese off a bagel and plowed through the toy closet.

His coffee-brown eyes seized upon a new gadget. "What's this?"

"Some sort of transformer toy."

His eyebrows drew into little raven wings as he dropped to the floor, completely absorbed. He'd transform it or tear it up trying. He experienced the totality of things before I could locate my glasses to see what it was. Our first major dispute came when he begged to go back to "The Lemon Store." I was clueless. Months later when we passed a Dairy Queen, he bounced and beamed and pointed it out. The red DQ logo doesn't represent a lemon, but it sure looks like one. Over our chocolate dipped cones, Eli gave me a sticky hug, and quipped, "See, Gee-Gee, now you know."

The fateful weigh-in morning, we left in a cold drizzle. I pulled up the hood of the child's parka and slipped into a cardigan I could shed before facing the scales.

"Are you snug?"

"As a bug," he piped, yanking the end of his seatbelt. "Why do you put my car seat in the middle? Mom lets me sit on the side."

"I like seeing your handsome face in the mirror," I said, thinking *and you're less apt to fling open the back door*.

"Okay, but I'm old enough to sit on the side. I have a loose tooth."

"You stop that growing right this minute," I teased and flipped the wipers on high as we turned onto the neighborhood street. His fist disappeared in his mouth wiggling said tooth. "Rain is bouncing off the windshield, Eli. That means it's turning into sleet."

"Why is it called sleet?"

"That's rain when it freezes—my, it's getting thick."

His hand shot out of his mouth and groped toward the door. "I'll let the window down."

"No, don't do that!" We gained the highway, but the wipers no longer cleared the windshield. "Let's go back home, I'm not driving to town in this. The road could get slippery—"

On cue, our car slid. We were barely going thirty, but thirty out of control is terrifying. We skated over into the oncoming lane, on an inexorable course with a white car rounding the curve.

I screamed. A stutter of traction transmitted to the steering wheel and the front tires caught. Taillights flashed across my rear-view mirror as we fish-tailed back to our side of the road and slushed into a driveway. I turned to find Eli gaping bug-eyed out the windshield. "Oh, darling, are you hurt?"

His face exploded into a grin. He bounced and pointed in front of the car. "Did you see it, Gee-Gee?" he yelled, "Did you see it?"

"See what?"

"The angel! Didn't you see the angel that pushed our cars apart?" Disappointment descended on him. "You didn't see it."

"No," I said, "my eyes were closed, but I don't doubt you." What better explanation for the white car sitting safely in the ditch *behind* us. "I'll go check on that driver. Stay in your seat-belt and I'll let down your window."

"Okay. I hope she won't have blood on her."

Unhurt, the woman said, "I don't know how I missed you—you were in my lane."

Eli was thrilled at the police car. "It was an angel," he reported, as the officer took notes. "Big, really big. It did like this—" The child made a sweeping motion with his arm. "—and pushed the cars apart."

I paid the other car's towing, then took my grand-child and frayed nerves home. After naptime, we walked to a nearby schoolyard. He sprinted down the soccer field but halted halfway and fled back toward me, screaming, "*Look*!" He ran into my arms, his heart jumping like a bunny rabbit. Both arms flailed skyward. One shaft of pure, crystalline light pierced the overcast, low-hanging clouds.

Eli straightened importantly. "That's the angel that pushed our cars apart." He crushed me in a hug. "See, Gee-Gee, now you know."

Chapter 33

Where Buzzards Roost

W hen I was little, Daddy would hoist me onto his shoulders and say, "Let's me and you go to the *gristle*."

He would smile at my baby word for the train trestle we crossed on the dirt road behind our middle Georgia homestead. A thin, intense man, Daddy worked tirelessly and found little to smile about. Mama said World War II changed him, but he never talked about it.

In the middle of the gristle one day, I cowered at the sight of vultures spinning overhead. I clung onto Daddy for dear life. "Let go of my go-fetch-it," he grumbled, prying my fingers off his Adam's apple. He set me down on a crosstie and rested on one knee beside me. "They live over there at Buzzard's Roost." He pointed to a tall stand of scraggly trees beside the river gorge. "Don't be afraid, they're just going home from work."

I understood that. Daddy went to work in town every day and came home at night.

"Turkey buzzards have a big job," he said, "and they do it very well."

ოჳოჳ

Fifty years later, when Daddy went to live at The Georgia War Veterans Home, this memory came back to me. Buzzard's Roost was the name of the water tower outside his building. At sundown, the old soldiers, some not so old, men and women in various stages of mobility, gathered at the glass end of the corridors to watch the birds.

With military precision, entire squadrons of vultures winged in. Early comers settled on the tip-top of the water tank. Others dotted the steel framework of the tower and seemed to group into families. Stragglers, like ticket holders, searched for designated seats and made a ruckus to oust gatecrashers.

The gray tower blended into the sky until evening when it took on its outline of roosting vultures. The girders stood out like giant black Xs against the haze of streetlights. It struck me as macabre.

At first, I dreaded the lobby lined with wheelchairs, elevators clogged with walkers, and halls echoing pain. Soon, I was stopping to admire the ever-changing bows a WAC wore in her hair and looking forward to sharing the elevator with a Marine who dubbed his walker as a "four-wheeler." The mantra of an invalid next door to Daddy, "…ace…ace…pair of eights…go on and kill me…you know you're going to…" was heart-wrenching when I learned he'd been a prisoner of war. Whether broken in body or mind, these men and women were survivors. They'd had a big job, and they had done it very well.

Surrounded by so many with war memories, Daddy no longer escaped his own. They emerged randomly in letters to his grandson who was serving in the army over-seas.

Germans had burp guns. When they fired it sounded just like somebody burped.

They had a hand grenade with a wood handle that we called a potato masher. Hand grenades were heavy, and I was always afraid I hadn't thrown them far enough.

One day we set out on a hike and I thought I stepped in a hole. I went down about five feet and found out the Germans had dug a trench and the snow filled it up.

I missed being at home three Christmases. I was at Ft. Bragg first and in England second and in Bremma Haven, Germany, third. At Christmas you think of home and loved ones.

When his grandson went to Iraq, Daddy remembered being twenty-three and marching across a foreign land, sleep-deprived and scared.

One morning we went to an English port directly across from France. We loaded our equipment on a landing craft, trucks in the bottom and jeeps on deck. I thought we could go that distance in about thirty minutes, but halfway we changed course and went up the coast to a large river. It was full of small boats that had been sunk, one right behind another. When the sun went down, I went below and slept in one of our trucks.

We came to a port called Le Havre that was so torn up by shells we had to pull up to a steep bank. We finally got unloaded and went about ten miles out in the country to a mansion in a big apple orchard. The only furniture in the house was two grand pianos. Sleeping on a floor was the worst way to sleep, but you don't have much choice when the snow is ten inches deep.

One night I dug a foxhole and we got shelled three times. Every time, I'd dig a little more, until next morning I was so deep my buddies had to pull me out. During combat I never got enough sleep. We'd move at night and then take an hour or two to dig our gun in, or we'd fire on crossroads ahead of us in case the Germans were bringing in reinforcements. It's a great blessing to lie down and go to sleep. Until the war ended, I was unable to do this.

When we came to rivers, we built rafts and pulled our Howitzer across. One night two of us were on a raft with the gun, right in the middle of a river, when the rope broke. It was way up in the middle of the next day before they got us across, but the Germans didn't catch us. It was so cold you didn't know how you could stand it.

He wrote about death with appalling detail.

The Germans took care of their wounded but expected civilians to bury the dead. There was a bad odor all during combat. It was a great relief after the war ended to be able to take a deep breath.

In the artillery, we were issued carbines, which were smaller and lighter than infantry rifles. After the war ended we manned road blocks and pulled guard duty. Two of us came up from the motor pool and were talking with a guard, when he shifted his carbine from one shoulder to the other. It caught in his jacket, fired, and hit the man with me in the neck. One minute he was talking and laughing, the next minute he was dead.

No wonder Daddy was so quick to allay my childhood fear. He was preparing me for a life filled with things much more fearsome than buzzards. It was a big job, and he did it very well.

About the Author

Genie Smith Bernstein began writing by falling out of the sky. After safely landing an airplane whose engine failed, she was unable to talk about the experience until capturing her emotions on paper. That exercise led to her ability to infuse writing with emotion.

Originally from Eatonton, Georgia, Bernstein writes in an authentic Southern voice. She makes her home in Athens, Georgia, and shares with her husband their joyously combined family of six children and fourteen globe-trotting grandchildren.

Bernstein is a featured columnist for *Georgia Connector*, Georgia's premier regional quarterly magazine. *Skating on the Septic Tank*, is a collection of her popular columns. Awarded South Carolina's Literary Award for Non-Fiction, her work has appeared in six anthologies.

Along with *Skating on the Septic Tank*, Bernstein's novel of Romantic Intrigue, *Act on the Heart* (plus reading group guide), is also published by Black Opal Books. The books are available through Amazon, the publisher, or Genie's website geniesmithbernstein.com.

Made in the USA
Columbia, SC
03 June 2019